# Weapons of Influence

# Weapons of Influence

## The Legislative Veto, American Foreign Policy, and the Irony of Reform

Martha Liebler Gibson

Westview Press

BOULDER • SAN FRANCISCO • OXFORD

*For Neil and Colin*

Copyright © 1992 by Westview Press, Inc.

Published in 1992 in the United States of America by Westview Press, Inc., 5500 Central Avenue, Boulder, Colorado 80301-2877, and in the United Kingdom by Westview Press, 36 Lonsdale Road, Summertown, Oxford OX2 7EW

A CIP catalog record for this book is available from the Library of Congress.
ISBN 0-8133-8600-4

Printed and bound in the United States of America

The paper used in this publication meets the requirements
of the American National Standard for Permanence of Paper
for Printed Library Materials Z39.48-1984.

10   9   8   7   6   5   4   3   2   1

# Contents

# Tables and Figures

# Acknowledgments

No book is ever written alone, and I gratefully acknowledge and thank the people who have made this one possible. I owe a particular debt to Lawrence C. Dodd, whose insights on Congress have proven invaluable to this work. Anne Costain, Steve Chan and Walter Stone have provided insightful comments, suggestions and encouragement from the inception of this project to its completion. My thanks as well to Professor Ronald Rogowski and the Department of Political Science at UCLA, where I was a visiting scholar while writing this book. The resources of that university were critical to its completion.

During the course of my research I interviewed numerous government officials and staff members. Since many wished to remain anonymous, I have omitted specific references to individuals when using interview material. My thanks to all of them.

Among those scholars who gave generously of their time and expertise along the many stages of this work, I would like to thank Louis Fisher and Ellen C. Collier, both of the Congressional Research Service, I. M. Destler, Roger Davidson, Barbara Craig, Jessica Korn, Warren Donnelley, George Holliday, Vladimir Pregelj, Morris Ogul and Joseph Cooper.

Amy Eisenberg and Jennifer Knerr, editors at Westview Press, expertly shepherded this book, and its author, through the editorial process. I am grateful for their skill and patience.

Finally my eternal thanks to Neil Gibson, partner and software engineer.

*Martha L. Gibson*
*Los Angeles*

# 1

## Introduction

In 1983 the Supreme Court ruled the legislative veto unconstitutional in the case *Immigration and Naturalization Service v. Chadha*. In doing so, the Court effectively used *legal* means to nullify one of the most important *political* accommodations between Congress and the executive in the twentieth century. The legislative veto modified eighteenth century governmental institutions to the needs of twentieth century policy making by fulfilling two important purposes: allowing congressional delegation of policy making authority to the executive while retaining congressional oversight of the ultimate use of that authority. In making its ruling, the Court may have addressed the constitutional questions surrounding the statutory mechanism, but left unresolved the political problems which led to its use in the first place. While the overriding outcome of the *Chadha* decision was predictable--contributing to the preservation of the dominant policy position held by the executive--there have also been important unforseen consequences resulting from the loss of the legislative veto. Analyzing a series of cases in foreign policy, this work argues that the loss of the legislative veto has, in certain cases, transformed the policy making *process* from one of grudging yet effective cooperation into one in which interbranch conflict is more likely if not inevitable.

### Governmental Structure in a Changing Nation

When the Founders wrote the American Constitution they were fully mindful that flexibility must be built into the document as it was impossible to foresee all exigencies which might arise in the development of the nation. Thus, though many powers are specifically delegated to

1

either the executive, legislature or judiciary, a number remain overlapping or vague. This "zone of twilight," it has been argued, was calculated by the Founding Fathers as "an invitation to struggle" over policy making influence.    Struggle would presumably stave off misguided or corrupt whims of a cloistered elite and ensure healthy debate as the nation hammered out the framework for the new democracy.

In the context of the eighteenth century the structure created was arguably very sound.   Based largely on an agrarian society and with foreign interests dominated by trade relations, crisis decision making was infrequent.  Debate within and among the branches was a hallmark of the new democratic system and proudly undertaken.

As American society progressed, however, the complexity of policy making changed the nature of the governing institutions, particularly Congress.  The legislature became professionalized as political powers shifted from state and local to national government.  Industrialization of the economy led to new dilemmas in both the social and economic spheres, and Keynsian economics gave government a new responsibility for managing the economic welfare of the nation and its people.  Torn between the desire to remain politically as well as geographically isolated from hostilities in Europe, and the recognition of growing international interdependence the United States wavered (sometimes dangerously) between isolationism and international involvement. The debate between the executive and legislative branches which had provided the fundamental character for the early American nation now became burdensome.  Legislators, recognizing their inability to maintain the same level of expertise on the growing number of complex issues requiring governmental action, increasingly delegated authority for action to the executive branch whose superior informational and staff resources were better equipped to handle them.

A series of factors, predominated by the economic crisis of the Great Depression, the dismal failure of the congressional isolationist policy between the World Wars, and the unprecedented American international position in the wake of World War II all led to a significant shift in the balance of institutional power away from Congress and toward the presidency. In the circumstances of the twentieth century legislators and presidents alike realized that in a growing number of areas the executive branch held the advantage in speed, information, expertise and secrecy which were vital to effective policy making.

But where did that leave the Congress?  Though by its own admission the executive was the more effective policy maker in *some* areas, legislators could not concede to a subordinate position in *all* policy decisions. Still, the mechanisms of governance and debate designed in the 1700's remained cumbersome in the 1900's. New means were needed in order to fulfill the dual goals of effective congressional participation in policy making without reintroducing the disadvantages and delays.

## Adapting the Tools to Govern

The legislative veto offered one viable solution which seemed to fulfill the requirements. It allowed Congress to delegate authority to the executive in a number of areas constitutionally relegated to the legislature but better handled by the executive. At the same time it reserved for Congress final authority over the policy outcome (should it choose to exercise it). From its original use in executive reorganization authority, hundreds of legislative veto provisions were included in domestic and foreign policy legislation. As the Founders had anticipated, the circumstances facing the nation in the twentieth century required modification of the tools provided in the eighteenth. Adding the legislative veto to the repertoire of statutory tools available to Congress allowed for increased efficiency in policy making without requiring either the abdication of the congressional role or unnecessary obstruction of the governmental process. It was a *political* solution to the problems of modern American government.

The feasibility of this new accommodation in governing relied primarily on comity between the branches. Congressional willingness to delegate combined with moderation and responsible action on the part of the executive were key. But as the presidency grew in strength, so did it become more covetous of its dominant policy making position. Evidence of this arose during the Truman, Eisenhower, Kennedy and Johnson Administrations, but came to a boiling point under Nixon. Now the legislative veto took on added significance. Where it previously allowed the legislature to *increase* the authority of the president via delegation, it now served a resurgent Congress as a means to *restrict* the imperious presidency and reestablish its role as codeterminor of governmental policy. The legislative veto was transformed from a tool of accommodation to a weapon of influence.

Though Congress had other tools at its disposal to assert its voice in policy making, the legislative veto lent a unique form of leverage. In its most liberal form, a single committee in either house could unilaterally kill an executive initiative. In a more conservative form a majority of both houses was required to defeat the executive initiative, but offered no recourse to the president. The legislative veto, once passed, was final.

The threat of its use, therefore, gave legislators (at times only small groups of legislators) considerable leverage to induce consultation during the formulation of policy, if not compromise on its substantive content. It created a context in which the executive's interests lay in reaching accommodation with legislators on controversial policy rather than facing a legislative veto.

In 1983, however, ruling in the case of *Immigration and Naturalization Service v. Chadha* the Supreme Court declared the legislative veto unconstitutional. Referring specifically to the one-house form of the veto, the Court argued that it breached constitutional standards of legislating by: 1) circumventing the bicameral requirement that *both* houses participate in the passage of legislation; and 2) denying the president the option to veto *de facto* legislation. Subsequent decisions also ruled the two-house, concurrent resolution form of the veto unconstitutional.

At the time of the ruling the usual battle lines formed. Proponents of congressional prerogatives decried the fundamental shift of powers toward the presidency which was expected to result from the decision. Advocates of a stronger presidency praised the ruling for restoring constitutionality to the governing process and allowing the president to fulfill his duties without the meddling of Congress.

Since the majority of legislative veto provisions had been written into domestic policy in order to oversee executive regulatory agencies, the attention of scholars, journalists and politicians focussed on *Chadha's* impact in that arena. What was unforseen, however, was the impact which the *Chadha* decision would have in foreign policy. Here too legislative vetoes were written into a variety of legislation in order to preserve some semblance of congressional influence. Foreign policy had shifted decisively toward the executive in the post-war period. And it was here, in the area of foreign policy, that Congress grappled to maintain a voice while allowing the executive the flexibility to conduct the day-to-day implementation. What observers failed to anticipate was the effect which *Chadha* would have as it presented Congress with the option of either acquiescing entirely in foreign policy, or finding different tools to reassert its disintegrating role.

The 1970s had been an era of congressional resurgence, and the legislature of the 1980s was in no mood to relinquish the gains it had made. Having lost the legislative veto representatives turned to a variety of alternatives, primarily report and wait provisions, hearings, joint resolutions of disapproval and direct counter-legislation to assert their views. But now the incentives in the game had changed. For the president, the incentive was no longer to consult (much less compromise) with Congress. Without the veto, any binding legislation enacted by

Congress was subject to presidential veto. Instead of needing a majority in both houses to support his initiatives, the president needed only one-third plus one in *either* house to avoid override and prevail. It was now in the president's interests to face down objections from the legislature, secure in the overwhelming probability of success.

While the impact which *Chadha* would have on the *outcome* of policy battles was not hard to predict, what was unforseen was the impact which the decision would have on the policy *process*. The alternatives which Congress has been forced to pursue have, in some instances, increased the profile of conflict between the branches of government. With the *Chadha* decision, Congress has lost a statutory weapon which allowed it to compel compromise in a low profile, often behind-the-scenes manner. By turning to hearings, joint resolutions of disapproval and counter-legislation, the policy conflicts between the branches have been brought into full public view. The result has been to infuse the process with inflammatory rhetoric, and undermine both domestic and international confidence in the coherence and stability of American foreign policy.

### American Foreign Policy After *Chadha*

One of the reasons that observers failed to anticipate the negative consequences of *Chadha* was the tendency to extrapolate too broadly from war powers. Though a legislative veto provision was written into the War Powers Resolution in 1973, Congress' demonstrated lack of will in enforcing the resolution has led critics to conclude that the veto's loss was meaningless. At the other extreme, scholars often noted the important role which the legislative veto had played in debates over arms sales to the Middle East, but treated this case as a unique outlier. Arguing that statutory alternatives could provide Congress with the same leverage, scholars ignored the lessons to be learned from this case and failed to appreciate its implications for foreign policy making in general.

In this work a typology of foreign policy issues and a theoretical framework are developed to explain the differential impact which *Chadha* has had across varying types of foreign policy issues. Using this framework, the case of arms sales to the Middle East is shown to be not merely an outlier, but representative of a class of foreign policy issues in which the legislative veto was critical to interbranch policy accommodation. By the same token, the typology demonstrates that war powers is a specific *type* of issue, and that extrapolation from this type of issue to *all* of foreign policy masks the real contribution of the legislative veto and hence the importance of its loss. As illustrated in Table 4.1 (Chapter 4), the impact of *Chadha* varies according to the nature of the issue type and the characteristics inherent to it which make conflict between the branches more or less likely. It will be argued that for those issue types which have the highest likelihood for conflict between the branches, Chadha has increased the profile of that conflict by eliminating Congress' means for compelling consultation and compromise in a low profile, behind the scenes manner.

Chapter 2 of this work will lay out the history of congressional-executive relations in the formulation of American foreign policy and trace the political circumstances which led to an increased reliance on the legislative veto. Chapter 3 discusses *Immigration and Naturalization Service v. Chadha*. It examines the Court's reasons for ruling the legislative veto unconstitutional and the theoretical implications of the decision for separation of powers and governmental performance. Chapter 4 lays out the typology of foreign policy issue and the theoretical framework for evaluating the impact of *Chadha* on the foreign policy making process. Specifically, it enumerates the conditions under which conflict between the branches is likely to occur based upon the varying types of foreign policy issues. It argues that the greater the likelihood of conflict between the branches, the greater the impact of *Chadha* on the policy process. Chapters 5 through 8 present qualitative and empirical evidence to analyze case studies which range among the various issue types. The case of arms sales to the Middle East illustrates the most dramatic impact of the *Chadha* decision. It represents a "strategic-salient" issue type. Nuclear non-proliferation policy, by contrast, is an example of a "strategic-nonsalient" issue. Most-favored-nation trade illustrates the impact of *Chadha* on "intermestic" issues. Finally, war powers is evaluated to illustrate the impact of *Chadha* on "crisis" issues. The final chapter, Chapter 9, presents conclusions from the research and discusses the policy implications of the *Chadha* decision and its impact on U.S. international relations.

The fundamental thesis of this work is that weapons matter. The range of statutory tools of influence available to Congress determines the relationship between the branches of government. Those who argue that the loss of the legislative veto has not significantly affected the policy process miss the nuance and subtleties which are critical to the choice of weapons legislators choose in their battle for policy participation. The legislative veto provided powerful leverage to Congress, allowing it to compel consultation and compromise from the executive. When that tool was taken away, Congress was forced to choose between acquiescence in foreign policy or a variety of tools which would require all out battle to influence policy. In those cases in which Congress has the motivation and will to oppose the president, the loss of the legislative veto has raised the profile of conflict between the branches and been a destructive influence on American foreign policy.

# 2

## Making American Foreign Policy: The Struggle for Influence

Chadha *didn't lessen the need for clearly stated arrangements of shared power between the executive and legislative branches on certain issues. It only significantly reduced our options for crafting those agreements.*

--Sen. Carl Levin (D-Mich.)

*The tools belong to the man who can use them.*

--Napoleon

In writing the American Constitution, the Founding Fathers intentionally overlapped the duties and functions of Congress and the president in foreign affairs. In Edward S. Corwin's famous words, the vague and ambiguous delineation of powers and prerogatives was an "invitation to struggle" over foreign policy, with a view, we now presume, to ensuring counselled debate, preventing reckless action which could embroil the new nation in the ubiquitous struggles of the European nations.

But the overlapping and intertwined powers delegated by the Constitution is only one source of confusion. The other is that so many critical functions are *not* specifically delegated in the document. From those powers which are explicitly delegated to one branch or the other a number of others have been *inferred*. This is the battleground where most of the interbranch "struggle" takes place.

The Constitution confers upon Congress the powers to: regulate commerce with foreign nations; declare war and grant letters of marque and reprisal and make rules concerning captures on land and water; to define and punish piracies and felonies committed on the high seas, and offenses against the law of nations; to raise and support armies; and to provide and maintain a navy (Article I, Section 8). To the Senate the Constitution delegates the power to ratify treaties and approve ambassadorial nominations (Article II, Section 2). To the President are delegated the powers of: Commander in Chief of the Army and Navy of the United States; to make treaties (subject to Senate advice and consent); to appoint ambassadors (subject to Senate advice and consent); and to receive ambassadors and other public ministers (Article II, Sections 2 and 3).

The Congress is charged "To make all laws which shall be necessary and proper for carrying into execution the foregoing powers, and all other powers vested by this Constitution in the government of the United States, or in any department or officer thereof" (Article I, Section 8). The President "shall take care that the laws be faithfully executed" (Article II, Section 3).

Controversy over the interpretation and limits of the foregoing powers has provided fodder to countless battles and numerous volumes. The classic debate between Alexander Hamilton and James Madison illustrates the propensity to draw significantly different conclusions from the document depending upon one's bias toward one branch or the other. To Hamilton, though Congress has the power to actually declare war, the president has the duty to preserve peace using "the 'executive power' to do whatever else the law of nations, co-operating with the treaties of the country, enjoin in the intercourse of the United States with foreign powers" (Schlesinger, 1973, 18). To Madison's reading, Congress' power to declare war included judgements concerning the context leading up to war. Congress, he argued, was not to be cornered by executive decisions concerning treaties or other executive actions which created "an antecedent state of things," making war unavoidable (Schlesinger, 1973, 19).

If two such contemplative men as Hamilton and Madison, themselves authors of the Constitution, could not agree on the document's meaning there was little hope that the ambiguities could be resolved by students two hundred years later. This, many argue, is the genius of the Constitution. Its meaning would only be defined as the nation lived under its provisions.

The constitutional roles of Congress and the president, defined by experience, have changed during the course of the nation's history. Though the Founders made a conscious attempt to prevent either the legislature or the executive from committing the nation to war without the genuine concurrence of the other, their efforts have failed. The actions of Presidents Tyler and Polk left Congress little option but to recognize a state of war with Mexico in 1846 once U.S. troops stationed antagonistically in the disputed land between Mexico and Texas were attacked. By the same token, congressional pressure was the decisive force in the War of 1812.

The power balance between the institutions depended on the interaction of two factors: the strength of the presidents in office; and the desire of Congress to assume a strong role in foreign policy. Predominance in foreign policy tended to be cyclical in nature. A period of dominance by one branch tended to be countered by a resurgence of the other. Lincoln's powerful expansion of presidential powers during the Civil War was met by a period of congressional power. It was during this period that Woodrow Wilson wrote his famous volume *Congressional Government* (1885). The congressional resurgence lasted until 1898, the Spanish-American war. From then until the end of World War I the president once again dominated foreign policy.

The heyday of congressional predominance in foreign affairs came in the period between the two World Wars. Traumatized by the experience of World War I, Congress led the nation in a policy of isolationism and neutrality. The prevailing mood of the time was symbolized by the Senate's failure to commit the United States to the League of Nations. But Congress was plagued by two outstanding failures during its term at the helm. Legislators, deliberating on the Treaty of Versailles introduced so many unacceptable amendments and conditions that President Wilson finally withdrew the treaty from consideration (Crabb and Holt, 1898, 14). The episode has since been held up as proof of Congress' irresponsibility in critical matters of foreign affairs. Perhaps more damning, however, was Congress' steadfast adherence to a policy of neutrality and isolationism in the face of encroaching fascism in Europe. Though the executive branch was, in fact, also split on the prospect of involving the United States in another foreign war, the overriding blame for American delay in coming to the Allies' aid lay at Congress' doorstep.

Despite serious congressional rebuke, Roosevelt agreed to sell Britain used American ships in return for the right to naval bases on its shores. The Lend-Lease Act was finally passed by Congress in March 1941, but only with the proviso that Congress could repeal the agreement at any time by concurrent resolution. Access to the legislative veto had made a political accommodation possible, as a reluctant Congress gave Roosevelt what amounted to an American commitment to the Allies in the war in Europe. As many presidents after him would do, Roosevelt objected to the constitutionality of the veto provision but signed the act. As Hitler's advance through Europe confirmed the very real threat which Europe faced, Congress' judgement in foreign policy was again discredited. The country looked to the president to lead it through the crisis of war.

Unlike previous periods in history, however, the ending of World War II did not bring a return to congressional dominance. The Depression and New Deal had fortified and expanded the role of the presidency in domestic policy. More dramatically, however, the emergence of the United States as a world power brought an entirely new set of responsibilities and complexities. Scarred by the failure of its neutrality policy, Congress was reluctant to take the lead role in determining American policy. The president remained the foremost power in American foreign policy--a role which would take on extraordinary dimensions in the decades to come.

## The Foreign Policy of a Superpower:
## The U.S. After WWII

The aftermath of World War II saw a unique convergence of circumstances which created an unprecedented unity of purpose in the United States. The United States had emerged from the war the dominant economic and military power in the world. In the preceding fifteen years, power in both domestic policy and foreign policy had shifted markedly toward the executive as Roosevelt tackled first the worst economic depression the country had ever faced and then the advent of global warfare (Schlesinger, 1959, 1960; Sundquist, 1981; Ambrose, 1988). Looking to the executive for leadership in defining the nation's new international role was hardly a surprising reaction to the times.

Though he later came to regret the words, then-Chairman of the Senate Foreign Relations Committee, William Fulbright (D-Ark.) wrote at the time:

> The price of democratic survival in a world of aggressive totalitarianism
> is to give up some of the democratic luxuries of the past. We should do
> so with no illusions as to the reasons for its necessity. It is distasteful
> and dangerous to vest the executive with powers unchecked and
> unbalanced. My question is whether we have any choice but to do so
> (Fulbright, 1961, 1).

The unity of purpose in foreign policy was cemented by the recognition of a clear and common enemy: communism, embodied primarily in the Soviet Union, though China would soon become another nemesis. Thus while congressional support of executive leadership is not surprising, what is surprising is the extent to which both Roosevelt and

Truman were able to extend their powers beyond what many considered reasonable bounds. "Although actual hostilities had lasted for less than four years, Roosevelt and Truman exercised emergency and war powers for more than twelve years" (Fisher, 1989, 7).

Congressional resentment, particularly among Republicans, of Roosevelt's cavalier attitude and failure to consult to any significant degree with Congress in either domestic or foreign policy led in part to the Legislative Reorganization Act of 1946. The overriding goal of the act was to restructure the institution of Congress in order to enhance its effectiveness as a policy making body and power vis-a-vis the president. As the Joint Committee on the Organization of Congress put it,

> the decline of Congress in relation to the executive branch of our Federal Government has caused increased legislative concern. Under the Constitution, Congress is the policy making branch of government. There are manifest growing tendencies in recent times toward the shift of policy making power to the executive, partly because of the comparative lack of effective instrumentalities and the less adequate facilities of the legislative branch. To redress the balance and recover its rightful position in our governmental structure, Congress, many Members feel, must modernize its machinery, coordinate its various parts, and establish the research facilities that can provide it with the knowledge that is power (cited in Fisher, 1989, 8).

Aware of congressional resentment over its second-class role, Truman began his administration attempting to increase the profile of congressional-executive consultation and put forward the appearance of unified policy making. Though he faced a Republican Congress, his efforts were reciprocated by the bipartisan beliefs and powerful influence of Senator Arthur Vandenberg (R-Mich.).

Truman was also aware that congressional control over the funds necessary to carry out a number of his foreign policy plans made congressional support indispensable. Consultation over the Truman Doctrine (aid to Greece and Turkey) and the Marshall Plan in 1947-48, and even the drafting of the NATO Treaty in 1949 appeared to mark a renewed cooperation between the branches in the formulation of American foreign policy (Tananbaum, 1987; Purvis, 1984). A close look at the substance of congressional participation reveals, however, that while a number of provisions designed to maintain a congressional role in the determination of American participation in NATO were incorporated, the wording was so vague as to make them weak in practice. One example was the rewording of the provision that each signatory was required to take "military and other action" should one of the others be attacked. It was changed to require that each nation would take "such action as it deems necessary...in accordance with their respective constitutional processes" (Tananbaum, 1987, 40). Yet debate over the proper "constitutional process" has raged since the time of Washington, and this provision did nothing substantive to clarify Congress' role in determining U.S. participation in NATO.

Still, members of Congress were mollified. As Senator Tom Connally (D-Tex.) put it, senators appreciated the opportunity to express their views while the treaty was being drafted rather than having "a finished document stuck under (their) noses" (cited in Tananbaum, 1987, 40).

The honeymoon ended in 1950 when Truman unilaterally decided to send American troops to Korea. Though he did meet a few times with legislators, those meetings were to inform Congress of actions already taken. In one instance, the decision to send ground troops was announced *during* his meeting with members of Congress (Paige, 1968; Tananbaum, 1987). When leaders of Congress objected, administration contempt of congressional meddling surfaced, as illustrated in the memoirs of then-Secretary of State Dean Acheson. He wrote:

> Senator Taft opened up in the Senate. His speech was typical--bitterly partisan and ungracious, but basically honest. The administration was responsible, he said, for the trouble that had overtaken it....The ground Senator Taft chose was typical senatorial legalistic ground for differing with the president, as we have seen earlier in the case of Senator Vandenberg. As a result, discussion in Congress of these differences is singularly lacking in understanding of substantive issues (Acheson, 1969, 410).

Contemplating later the decision not to gain congressional approval for the Korean action Acheson stood by the administration's original decision.

> To have obtained congressional approval, it has been argued, would have obviated later criticism of "Truman's war." In my opinion, it would have changed pejorative phrases, but little else....Nevertheless, it is said, congressional approval would have done no harm. True, approval would have done none, but the process of gaining it might well have done a great deal....The harm it could do seemed to me far to outweigh the little good that might ultimately accrue (Acheson, 1969, 413-415).

Resentment over Truman's Korea decision was compounded by his 1951 decision to send U.S. troops to Europe to participate in NATO forces under the command of General Dwight D. Eisenhower. The conflict which this decision touched off came to be known as the "Great Debate" over the limits of executive authority (Sundquist, 1981; Tananbaum, 1987).

Despite flamboyant rhetoric from some members of Congress and months of hearings, in the end little was actually done to rein in executive action. While Senator Taft (R-Ohio) argued that it was "incumbent upon the Congress to assert clearly its own constitutional powers unless it desires to lose them" numerous proposals for legislation which would constrain Truman to any serious degree were rejected (Fisher, 1989). In the end the Senate passed a sense-of-the-Senate resolution approving the troop deployment and requiring that all future actions be taken only with the approval of Congress. The House declined to pass a similar resolution, leaving the Senate resolution with no legally binding authority. The result was little more than Congress pleading to be included.

The Eisenhower Administration marked an exception to the jealous propriety over foreign policy evident in administrations before and after it. In the end, Eisenhower's style appears to have proven the wisdom of 'catching bees with honey.' Having witnessed the damaging effects which conflict between the executive and legislative branches had on international confidence in American foreign policy, Eisenhower argued that American policy would carry greater weight among both allies and enemies if presented as a unified front (Ambrose, 1988; Warburg, 1989; Fisher, 1989, 15). Testimony to the success of such a tack was Eisenhower's ability to defeat the Bricker Amendment which during Truman's time enjoyed strong bipartisan support. The amendment would have imposed restrictions upon presidential agreements so that they could not be used to evade limitations which Congress had put on executive treaties (Tananbaum, 1987, 43).

The real wisdom of Eisenhower's strategy was in gaining from Congress area resolutions which would allow him a large degree of flexibility of action regarding U.S. policy in a given region. Primary among these were: the Formosa Resolution (1955), which Eisenhower requested in order to defend the island of Formosa against the communist Chinese who had already threatened the Nationalist-held islands of Quemoy and Matsu; and the Middle East Resolution (1956) in which he requested the grant of authority to use American forces as he saw necessary to check Soviet expansionism in the Middle East (a topic of concern in the wake of the conflict over the Suez).

Confronted with such a candid opportunity to share responsibility for American foreign policy, legislators revealed considerable trepidation about their own ability to meet the challenge. New York Congressman Abraham Multer argued, "The buck has been passed to us by the president. Under the Constitution it is his duty and he has the power to make foreign policy." Californian James Roosevelt warned that Eisenhower was "virtually giving over to Congress power which properly does not belong to the Congress." William Colmer of Mississippi, whom Sundquist suggests "probably spoke for the House majority" said,

> We cannot make foreign policy in the Congress of the United States; that would be impossible. You know where that would lead to. So we must rely on the Chief Executive and those who would advise him. In fact,...it is the constitutional duty of the president to make our foreign policy (quotes cited in Sundquist, 1981, 116).

Such statements, though surprising, may be very revealing as concerns the true sentiments of legislators even today. Having been put in the position of generally fighting a strong uphill battle for even perfunctory consultation over foreign policy, rhetoric can be strong, sometimes even extreme, with little threat of making a difference. Faced with the actual prospect of taking responsibility for policy, however, members may well reveal similar reticence to that seen in 1956. This is not to say that members of Congress do not want a substantive voice in foreign policy. They do. Rather, it explains the countless episodes in which rhetoric has not been matched by action; when the chest-beating of Congress has resulted in legislation dying (with no apparent intent to resurrect it) merely because Congress goes into recess. What Congress wants is to be heard, to be considered. Edwards has noted that the "two presidencies" thesis of presidential dominance in foreign policy is really only persuasive under the Eisenhower Administration and less so under succeeding presidents (Edwards, 1986). That is because members of Congress, content that their institutional role was being taken seriously, were much more inclined to give this president flexibility in foreign policy. They wanted to be consulted and listened to, not necessarily to control policy. Eisenhower played Congress masterfully.

With the end of the Eisenhower Administration came the end of the "experiment" in congressional-executive cooperation in foreign policy (Fisher, 1989). Kennedy handled the Bay of Pigs disaster and the Cuban Missile Crisis unilaterally, and though Congress did pass the Cuba Resolution it was not an authorization of force, merely a sense of Congress. The notorious Gulf of Tonkin Resolution (South East Asia Resolution) of 1964, passed in part on the basis of the Johnson Administration's fabricated reports of attacks on American ships, showed the danger in delegating broad strokes of authority to a president less inclined to consider congressional sentiments than was Eisenhower. Where such resolutions had appeared to provide the ideal combination of congressional participation in broad foreign policy with flexibility of executive day-to-day management under Eisenhower, under Johnson they proved to be the vehicle to *prevent* meaningful congressional participation.

Johnson's commitment of American troops to the Dominican Republic, without congressional approval, convinced Senate Foreign Relations Committee Chairman J. William Fulbright (D-Ark.) that Congress needed to reestablish its legitimate role in foreign policy. This incident, not the Vietnam War, began the drive in Congress which would ultimately result in the War Powers Resolution in 1973. Though the events of the Vietnam War unquestionably deepened congressional mistrust of executive-dominated foreign policy, the "credibility gap" began as revelations emerged that Johnson had misled Congress concerning the threat to American lives in the Dominican Republic just as he had done with the Gulf of Tonkin. The chasm between what the president had led Congress to believe and the reality of international events had taken on shocking proportions. Where sins of omission had previously been the major source of incredulity, now Congress actively doubted the veracity of the president's word.

In 1967 Fulbright introduced a resolution declaring that national commitments of American forces could only be made through *both* congressional and executive action to pass legislation "specifically intended to give effect to such a commitment" (Fulbright, 1967, 1; Stennis and Fulbright, 1971, 47; Tananbaum, 1987, 48). Though the resolution inspired considerable discussion and debate, Congress failed to act on it until 1969 when a modified version, the National Commitments Resolution of 1969 was passed. Though the wording of the resolution was broad and encompassing, it too was passed merely as a sense-of-the-Senate resolution with no legally binding authority (Fisher, 1987, 17).

Despite the relatively feeble incentive value that the National Commitments Resolution contained in terms of compelling executive consultation and cooperation with Congress, it did set off a series of other measures all demonstrating the depth of congressional dissatisfaction with its diminished role in foreign policy. Among these were the Cooper Amendment, prohibiting the president from introducing ground troops into Laos--despite the fact that the only American activity in Laos at the time was air units, which were not prohibited--; the Cooper-Church Amendment, prohibiting ground troops--but not air strikes--in Cambodia; and the repeal of the Gulf of Tonkin Resolution, which Nixon did not oppose, arguing that he did not need it to authorize his actions (Sundquist, 1981, 247-252; Crabb and Holt, 1989, 141).

In June 1970 Senator Jacob Javits (R-N.Y.) introduced the War Powers Resolution. After years of debate, and compromise, the measure was finally approved in 1973. Nixon vetoed the War Powers Resolution, arguing that it was an unconstitutional infringement upon presidential powers as Commander-in-Chief. Congress overrode his veto November 7, 1973 by votes of 284-135 in the House, and 75-18 in the Senate (Crabb and Holt, 1989). Symbolically and substantively, the resolution was the hallmark of the congressional resurgence of the 1970s.

### The Reassertive Congress

Post-war confidence in the necessity of strong presidential leadership had allowed the powers of the presidency to get out of control. The imperial president needed to be checked. Congress set out to regain its position as a partner in foreign policy.

Congress' ability to regain its prerogatives in a broad range of policy areas was critically aided by a political evolution which had been in the making since the late 1950s. Significant gains for Democrats in the 1958 elections provided the basis for a key element in the reform movement in Congress overall: the Democratic Study Group (DSG). Democratic liberals sought to loosen the pivotal power of older, entrenched committee chairmen who subscribed to the dictum of presidential primacy in foreign affairs, and who had the ability to bury bills in a variety of ways. Ironically, these reformist Democrats were joined in support by Republican members who also had an interest in loosening the tight controls of the Democratic establishment (Whalen, 1982). Initiatives by the DSG led to the Legislative Reorganization Act of 1970 which decentralized committee chairman power (Dodd, 1977; Whalen, 1982).

At the same time, there was an unusual turnover in the congressional elections of the early 1970s which brought in a critical number of freshman members, many of whom shared a mistrust of the powerful presidency. The structural reforms brought about through the Legislative Reorganization Act of 1970 gave voice to members who advocated greater congressional activism in foreign policy, ultimately leading to the enactment of the War Powers Resolution in 1973. The Madisonian/Hamiltonian debate over which branch should have primacy in international affairs had been rekindled.

While the structural reforms provided the potential for meaningful participation by Congress in foreign policy, the legislative veto was the primary tool used to transform that potential into action. Striking mainly in the areas of foreign aid, arms sales, trade and war powers, Congress sought to make itself a force to be reckoned with. Congress could use the threat of a legislative veto to compel the president into consultation and compromise. It was clearly in the president's interests to resolve conflict *before* the finalization of deals with foreign nations. The embarrassment of having Congress veto an executive initiative, coupled with the damage such an event would do to the legitimacy of future international agreements was a powerful incentive for cooperation.

Legislative veto provisions have since been included in hundreds of acts by Congress.[1] Among the more notable in the area of arms sales is the 1974 Nelson-Bingham Amendment to the Foreign Military Sales Act of 1968[2] which requires the president to give formal notice to Congress of any proposed military equipment sales exceeding $25 million. It further provides Congress the ability to block any such proposed sale by concurrent resolution. The restrictions in Nelson-Bingham were tightened in 1981 by an amendment to the Arms Export Control Act (PL 94-329) which lowered the "tripwire" for notification from $25 million to $7 million, drastically increasing the number of executive initiatives which fell under the requirement.

For Congress, these provisions ensured a measure of control over a process in which they had long been little more than spectators. At very least they compelled consultation between the executive and legislative branches and raised Congress' credibility as a serious participant in the foreign policy process. Still, Congress was aware that its role could become obstructionist if careful consideration was not made of extenuating circumstances which may face the nation, requiring fast action by the president. With this in mind amendments were introduced which intentionally retained presidential flexibility in certain circumstances. The Arms Export Control Act and the International Security Assistance Act of 1979, for example, contain provisions allowing the president to waive the requirement for congressional notification of a major arms sale on grounds of national security. He is, however, required to provide "a detailed justification for his determination, including a description of the emergency circumstances which necessitate the immediate issuance of the letter of offer [to the recipient country] and a discussion of the national security interests involved" (PL 96-92).

Similarly, the 1981 Foreign Aid Bill includes a section allowing the president to waive most legal restrictions (subject to the legislative veto) on foreign aid and arms sales if he notifies Congress that doing so "is vital to the national security interests of the United States." The president "shall consult with, and shall provide a written policy justification to the congressional foreign policy and appropriations committees" (PL 96-533).

These examples clearly show that Congress is not only mindful of the dangers inherent in excessive restrictions upon the president but actively took steps to mitigate their effects. In essence the attempt was made to strike a balance between viable mechanisms of control and dangerous impediments to national security.

But Congress' ability to use the legislative veto to reassert its role in foreign policy ended in 1983 when the Supreme Court, ruling in *Immigration and Naturalization Service v. Chadha*, determined the one-house form of the legislative veto (and by implication its companion forms) to be unconstitutional. Their decision was fortified two weeks later in other cases which held the two-house form of the congressional veto unconstitutional as well. The decision was analyzed primarily for the impact which it would have on domestic policy since the majority of vetoes were written into domestic legislation and since the only exercise of the congressional veto had come in domestic policy. Far less consideration was given to the impact which *Chadha* would have in foreign policy. Though Congress never actually used the veto to kill an executive initiative in foreign policy, the loss of the legislative veto would have significant ramifications in congressional-executive relations in this critical area of policy.

## The Role of the Courts

Over the course of American history, some of the questions concerning the institutional balance in foreign policy have been addressed by the courts. The continuing struggle between Congress and the president, however, is testimony to the fact that even the Supreme Court has not been effective in settling disputes over the constitutional delegation of powers in foreign affairs. Part of this is intentional on the Court's part, part of it is evasion.

A number of cases have been brought before the courts to determine whether Congress has the right to delegate foreign policy authority to the president, and in turn whether once delegated, the Congress has any further claim on the use of that authority. The courts have taken two approaches to such questions. One has been to decide the cases on the basis on congressional *intent*. That is, derive Congress' position on an issue through explicit statements, legislation on related or similar matters, legislative history, or implicit consent through inaction (Glennon, 1990, 14). The second approach to questions of institutional prerogatives in foreign policy has been to determine the issue "non-justiciable" based upon the "political questions" doctrine. The political questions doctrine, first brought into use in *Marbury v. Madison* (1803) removes questions from judicial resolution by categorizing them as inherently political in nature, and thus reconcilable only by the political branches (the legislative and the executive) themselves. Not until the *Chadha* decision had the Court ruled directly on the constitutionality of legislative veto provisions, and even that case pertained to domestic legislation with only secondary consideration given to the impact which it may have on foreign policy.

It should be noted that the courts have never ruled against Congress in a case determining foreign policy powers. As constitutional scholar Michael Glennon notes,

> In no case touching on foreign relations has the Supreme Court invalidated acts of Congress because it impinged upon the president's sole power under the Constitution. In two hundred years of dispute between the president and Congress over war and peace, commitments and neutrality, trade embargoes and arms sales, Congress has never lost before the High Court (Glennon, 1990, 13).

But this does not mean that Congress has not been damaged by the Court's *failure to decide*. Indeed, ruling numerous cases non-justiciable in recent years has had a powerful political effect. By ruling that the political branches must settle questions between themselves, the advantage is lodged with the more powerful branch, which in the postwar era has been the executive. Though it is difficult to prove definitively, it can plausibly be argued that indeed the courts have taken on a highly political role in the foreign policy struggle by ruling questions nonjusticiable. Many of the questions revolve around issues identical to those which earlier courts had found cause to adjudicate. A brief look at some of the landmark cases in foreign policy powers will help to illustrate the point.

## *Little v. Barreme*

In the case *Little v. Barreme* (1804) the question before the court was whether a navy captain, George Little, could be prosecuted for the capture of a Danish vessel, the Flying Fish, during an undeclared naval war between the United States and France in 1799. Little argued that he was following orders from his superior, the Secretary of the Navy, to stop ships which might be trying to evade an embargo. In the Non-Intercourse Act of 1799 Congress authorized naval officers to stop and search American ships which they had reason to suspect were bound for a French port. If the ship was in fact headed for France, the ship could then be confiscated and sold or auctioned (Schlesinger, 1973; Glennon, 1990). The orders sent by the Secretary of Navy expanded the original congressional authorization to allow for seizure of ships which were *suspected* of being American, and were either *bound toward* or *headed from* a French port. The Flying Fish was a Danish ship sailing away from a French port. The owners of the Flying Fish thus brought suit for the seizure.

In the end, the court ruled that Captain Little was liable for exceeding the authority granted in the Non-Intercourse Act. The critical message for the purposes of congressional-executive powers in foreign policy was that it upheld the right of Congress to impose restrictions on executive action in foreign affairs. Where there were no prior restrictions guiding presidential action, the court held, the president enjoyed independent power to protect American rights and interests abroad. Where Congress had set guidelines for action, however, the president is obliged to abide by those guidelines (Schwartz, 1981; Glennon, 1990).

> [Justice John Marshall's] decision [in *Little v. Barreme*] seems to presuppose that congressional authorization of a specific scope of executive action is an implicit denial to the President of authority to order action outside that scope...[and] thus sets the stage for direct confrontation between the executive and legislative branches over foreign affairs (Glennon, 1990, 7).

## *Youngstown Sheet & Tube Company v. Sawyer*

In the 1953 *Youngstown Sheet & Tube Company v. Sawyer* case, also known as the Steel Seizure Case, the Court blocked President Truman's attempt to use emergency powers during the Korean War to seize a domestic steel mill when steel workers went on a nationwide strike. He argued that steel production was critical to the war effort and thus on the grounds of national security governmental seizure of the steel mill was part of his executive powers (Neustadt, 1960; Schlesinger, 1973; Glennon, 1990). The Court disagreed, arguing that the president's action was in effect lawmaking. In his opinion on the case, Justice Hugo Black wrote, "The power, if any to issue the order must stem either from an act of Congress or from the Constitution itself" (343 U.S. 585 [1952]).

The more critical comments for institutional prerogatives in foreign policy, however, came in the concurring opinion written by Justice Jackson. In it, Jackson spelled out the framework for the branches to reach a cooperative use of their concurrent powers, but one which would be based upon congressional action to guide presidential prerogatives (much like the philosophy in *Little*). Jackson wrote:

Presidential powers are not fixed but fluctuate, depending upon their disjunction or conjunction with those of Congress....When the president acts pursuant to an express or implied authorization of Congress, his authority is at its maximum, for it includes all that he possesses in his own right plus all that Congress can delegate....When the president acts in absence of either a congressional grant or denial of authority, he can only rely upon his own independent powers, but there is a zone of twilight in which he and Congress may have concurrent authority, or in which its distribution is uncertain....In this area, any actual test of power is likely to depend on the imperatives of events and contemporary imponderables rather than on abstract theories of law....When the president takes measures incompatible with the expressed or implied will of Congress, his power is at its lowest ebb, for then he can rely only upon his own constitutional powers minus any constitutional power of Congress over the matter (343 U.S. 579, 635-38 [1952] Jackson, J., concurring).

At bottom, in the case of disagreement over the appropriate course of action, the ruling makes it incumbent upon the president to either refrain from action or gain sufficient congressional support for his initiatives (Koh, 1988).

At the same time, however, Jackson warned Congress that the power to maintain a voice in policy was ultimately its own, and not the Court's responsibility.

I have no illusion that any decision by this court can keep power in the hands of Congress if it is not wise and timely in meeting its problems. A crisis that challenges the president equally, or perhaps primarily, challenges Congress....We may say that power to legislate for emergencies belongs in the hands of Congress, but only Congress itself can prevent power from slipping through its fingers (343 U.S. 579, 635-38 [1952] Jackson, J. concurring).

These two cases, *Little v. Barreme* and *Youngstown Sheet & Tube Co.*, serve as precedents for the limitation of executive action in foreign policy. Another case, however, *Curtiss-Wright*, has been interpreted as a counterweight, a vindication of presidential power in foreign affairs.

## United States v. Curtiss-Wright Export Corporation

In 1934 Congress had passed a joint resolution authorizing President Roosevelt to impose an arms embargo (by executive proclamation) to stop the sale of arms to Bolivia and Paraguay who were at that time fighting the Chaco War (Schlesinger, 1973). The Curtiss-Wright Export

Corporation was discovered in a conspiracy to violate the embargo, and thus brought to court. In its defense, Curtiss-Wright Corp. argued that the embargo was invalid since the delegation of authority from Congress to the president was unconstitutional in the first place.

In its ruling the Court held that the delegation of authority *was* constitutional, and that moreover, the president was acting through executive powers which are not subject to challenge from the legislature ("plenary" powers). Justice Sutherland wrote:

> It is important to bear in mind that we are here dealing not alone with an authority vested in the president by an exertion of legislative power, but with such an authority plus the very delicate and exclusive power of the president as the sole organ of the federal government in the field of international relations--a power which does not require as a basis for its exercise an act of Congress, but which, of course, like every other governmental power, must be exercised in subordination to the applicable provisions of the Constitution (299 U.S. 319-20 [1936]).

Not only has this decision appalled some of the most prominent historians and legal scholars of our time (Schlesinger, 1973; Koh, 1988; Glennon, 1990; Henkin, 1990) but the Founders would have found perplexing the dual assertions that powers must be subordinate to the Constitution while at the same time calling the executive the "sole organ of the federal government in international relations."[3] But for better or worse, the decision has served as the basis of argument for a broad range of unilateral executive actions in foreign affairs. Even Lt. Col Oliver North invoked the *Curtiss-Wright* case during the Iran-Contra hearings to justify covert actions in Central America (Glennon, 1990, 21).

Despite clear precedents for judicial consideration of cases involving the relative constitutional powers of Congress and the president in foreign policy, the Court has made it a frequent practice in recent years to judge a large number of cases nonjusticiable on political grounds. Many of these cases have dealt with similar questions to those addressed in previous judicial decisions, such as the president's ability to unilaterally terminate a defense treaty (*Goldwater v. Carter*); whether a bilateral agreement made by the executive conflicted with existing congressional legislation (*Cranston v. Reagan*); the president's right to keep troops abroad despite congressional declarations and legislation requiring withdrawal (*Crockett v. Reagan*); or to report to Congress on the activities of military personnel abroad (*Lowry v. Reagan*). By not ruling on these cases the Court has effectively strengthened the status quo, which in the era of the imperial presidency has been a blow to congressional reassertion. As Justice Jackson warned, Congress will clearly have to rely upon its own devices in its efforts to regain influence in foreign policy. The courts are an unlikely ally.

## American Foreign Policy
## Without the Legislative Veto

Initially, some observers hailed a new era of codetermination and cooperation in U.S. foreign policy making while others decried the congressional intrusion as unconstitutional, obstructionist and dangerous. After a series of battles, however, both branches learned to accommodate themselves to the new rules of the game.

> The revolutionary zeal that broke up much of Nixon's and Ford's foreign policy now began to be harnessed for building better institutions and instruments of systematic codetermination....Congress had gained the right to be consulted...*before* key decisions were made or policies implemented [emphasis original](Franck and Weisband, 1979, 82-84).

Having lost the leverage of the legislative veto, Congress has become considerably more wary of the president's unfettered authority in foreign affairs. The *Chadha* decision had taken away a unique weapon in the struggle over foreign policy. It had set legal limits on congressional recourse to executive action, but had not resolved the political causes of conflict.

At the time some observers argued that the decision would not significantly affect congressional efforts to participate in foreign policy decisions (Gilmour and Craig, 1984; Fisher, 1985). They cited a variety of alternatives, such as the joint resolution of disapproval or appropriations restrictions, which would accomplish the same effect as the legislative veto. The argument of this work is that while other options are indeed available, none is able to reconstruct the delicate balance gained through the combination of flexibility and security which the legislative veto offered. Instead, having lost the capacity to redirect or annul executive initiatives, Congress has been forced to take higher profile, more conflictive action in order to affect policy.

The *Chadha* decision left Congress with a choice between returning to its role as merely a facilitator of presidential initiatives in foreign policy or adopting alternative means of control. To maintain its hard-fought gains in the codetermination of foreign policy Congress has turned primarily to joint resolutions of disapproval and restrictions on appropriations. In certain areas of foreign policy, these alternatives have proven more conducive to conflict than cooperation. In fact, they have led to a structure in which conflict is unavoidable and cooperation difficult, even if desirable.

Ironically, the ultimate effect of the *Chadha* decision has been to increase congressional obstruction of the president in foreign policy rather than decrease it. Not all areas of foreign policy have been affected in the same manner. In war powers, for example, the loss of the legislative veto has had little if any effect. In arms sales to the Middle East, by contrast, it has had a severely detrimental effect. The critical difference is the nature of the issue under consideration and the potential it holds for interbranch conflict. In those cases where interbranch conflict is the most likely, the *Chadha* decision has raised the profile of that conflict and made it more destructive to the foreign policy process.

Instead of lessening congressional encroachment in what many view as presidential prerogatives in foreign affairs, Congress has been forced to adopt constitutionally acceptable means of control. These alternatives have introduce greater conflict into the structure of congressional-executive interaction. It is clear that Congress has no intention of voluntarily returning itself to its post-war position of junior partner in foreign policy. For better or worse, it is determined to use the means at its disposal to maintain as much control as possible. Unfortunately, the means at its disposal *post-Chadha* create a context of interaction which is considerably more conflictive than that afforded by the legislative veto. As veteran congressional scholar James Sundquist has noted, "the president and Congress are compelled to live together in a marriage arranged by matchmakers of a long-gone era, a marriage that, however loveless, is without the possibility of divorce" (Sundquist, 1976). The critical question, then, is not whether there should be codetermination, but how to minimize conflict. Striking down the legislative veto was not the answer.

# 3

# The Fall of the Legislative Veto: *I.N.S. v. Chadha*

The legislative veto was a political accommodation between Congress and the president designed to serve a dual purpose: effective policy making and the preservation of congressional oversight. As the policy demands of the nation grew in number and complexity it allowed Congress to delegate authority to the executive branch to carry out functions which were originally delegated to the legislature but which the executive branch was now better suited to handle. At the same time, Congress reserved the right to review the use of the delegated authority and disapprove actions in the case of abuse or malfeasance.

But the legislative veto also served another, less pristine purpose. It allowed Congress to avoid responsibility for legislating in politically sensitive areas, preferring to delegate both the authority and the blame to the executive. In oversight Congress was able to claim credit for killing politically unpopular policy initiatives without the burden of offering viable alternatives.

At best the legislative veto was an eminently logical accommodation to the complexities of modern government--precisely the kind of adaptation to contemporary circumstances which the Founders had in mind when they designed our system of government. At worst it was a facilitator of legislative irresponsibility, a means to transfer the duties of elected representatives to unaccountable unelected administrators.

The legislative veto was originally formulated in 1932 to allow Herbert Hoover to reorganize the executive branch without requiring congressional approval at every step. Its use steadily grew in the '40s, '50s and '60s, and then took a dramatic jump in the 1970s. Once viewed as a valuable release mechanism which Congress could use to unload some of the overwhelming burden of legislating, in the era of the imperial presidency it also became a tool of restriction. As the power balance between the branches shifted decisively toward the president Congress groped for a means to maintain a voice in policy making. Though the looming power of the executive can be traced partly to Congress' own acquiescence and unwillingness to assume responsibility in a broad range of policy areas, the legislature had lost more control than it had planned. Cavalier actions, primarily by President Nixon, in impoundment, price controls, abuse of national intelligence, the secret war in Cambodia, and, of course, Watergate, stunned legislators into the realization of exactly how far they had let the executive stray.

The goal was not to take back all of the authority which Congress had delegated to the executive, for the complexities of governing still remained. The goal was effective oversight and limitation. The legislative veto offered Congress a means to recapture influence without losing the advantages of delegation.

## Forms and Functions of the Legislative Veto

The legislative veto took a number of forms ranging from a veto by a single committee chairperson to a concurrent resolution requiring two-thirds of each house.[4]  The form of veto chosen varied with the nature of the issue under consideration (Cooper and Hurley, 1983). As could be expected, some forms of the veto offered an enormous amount of leverage to single committees or subcommittees (or in one case to a single committee chairperson) while other forms relied upon a broader range of congressional support.  Likewise, differing forms of the veto offered greater or lesser amounts of leverage to the executive in the effort to stave off congressional action.

A provision which allowed for a single committee or subcommittee, or even the chairperson of that committee, to nullify executive action clearly offered the greatest leverage to individual legislators. These forms of the veto made no pretense of reflecting the consensus of the entire Congress, allowing a single individual or small group of individuals to dictate the survival of a given executive initiative.  (In practice the committee chairperson veto had only been used once, in a 1953 supplementary appropriations bill [Cooper and Hurley, 1983, 7]).  While single committee vetoes had been included in various pieces of legislation over the years, it had never been among the more popular forms of the congressional veto.

Much more common was a provision which allowed a joint committee, dual committees, or multiple committees (in either or both houses) to veto an initiative. Though this form still did not profess to engage the entire Congress in consideration of a given program, it did widen the scope of congressional participation somewhat. Clearly, however, this form still gave an enormous amount of power to a select few and gave the legislature considerable power to compel consultation from the executive branch--particularly executive agencies (Bruff and Gellhorn, 1977). Committee vetoes could be either affirmative or negative, the former requiring congressional committee approval in order for an initiative to take effect, the latter allowing an initiative to take effect *unless* the committee disapproved it. In certain instances of congressional uncertainty or sluggishness, the disapproval form could actually work to the advantage of an executive agency (Bruff and Gellhorn, 1977).

One-house vetoes, or simple resolutions, allowed either house to nullify an initiative or program. Unlike committee vetoes, one-house vetoes have always taken the negative form. The one-house veto still lent significant leverage to the legislature since any effort to avoid negative action required the executive to secure the support of *both* houses.

Two-house vetoes, or concurrent resolutions, required both houses to kill an executive initiative. As with committee forms of the veto, the two-house form could be either affirmative or negative. Though the two-house veto still provided Congress with a significant tool of influence, the leverage capability of the these two sub-forms varied greatly. The two-house negative veto could be averted even if the executive was able to gain the support of only one of the houses. The two-house affirmative veto, by contrast, put the burden on the executive to gain the support of *both* houses. In this circumstance, an initiative could not go into effect until it had received approval from both houses, thus it was the functional equivalent of the one-house veto since either house could fail to support the initiative and thus kill it. Though it was relatively more difficult for Congress to pass this form, the power of the two-house veto should not be dismissed, particularly on controversial issues. It still provided the legislature with a unique tool to compel consultation from the executive.

Other types of legislative vetoes included combinations of those mentioned above. Most forms of the veto included a report-and-wait provision which did not allow an initiative, program or agency rule to go into effect until it had been before Congress for a given period of time (usually anywhere from 5 to 90 days). During this waiting period the appropriate legislative action could be taken to either approve or disapprove the proposal. In many cases Congress' failure to act within the specified time period was interpreted as implicit approval. While it has been argued that in a few cases delay negatively affected an agency proposal (Bruff and Gellhorn, 1977), the report-and-wait provision itself was not the mechanism of veto. Report-and-wait provisions which then require either committee approval or a joint resolution of disapproval (disapproval by *both* houses which is then subject to presidential veto) have been a powerful force in the relationship between congressional committees and executive agencies (Cooper and Hurley, 1983). As will be discussed in the next section, because of the distributive (pork-barrel) nature of the programs under consideration, a number of scholars have argued that the legislative veto provided undue leverage to special interest groups (Bruff and Gellhorn, 1977; Dodd and Schott, 1979; Gilmour, 1982; Ethridge, 1984).

## Policy Influence

The use of the legislative veto has grown over the years, with a drastic increase in their use in the 1970s. Of the approximately 274 legislative veto provisions written into domestic and foreign policy statutes by 1980 more than half had been incorporated in the 1970s (Norton, 1976; Cooper and Hurley, 1983). Eighty legislative vetoes had been enacted between 1975 and 1978 alone (Schick, 1983, 176). Not only were the number of bills containing veto provisions growing, but the number of veto provisions contained in each bill also increased (Dodd and Schott, 1979, 232).

This comes as little surprise. The 1970s was the heyday of the imperial presidency and the era of the resurgent Congress. Where the legislative veto had previously been used as a tool of accommodation, it now became a weapon of restraint. Legislative veto provisions were written into such legislation as the Congressional Budget and Impoundment Control Act (1974) and the War Powers Resolution (1973) in direct reaction to the cavalier actions of President Nixon. As Table 3.1 demonstrates, most of the legislative veto provisions were in domestic policy, though a number were also written into foreign policy legislation.

Since 1932 Congress has passed 125 vetoes, all in domestic policy. Of those, 64 were rejections of presidential spending, 35 nullified agency regulations, programs or decisions, and 24 disapproved executive reorganization plans (Gilmour and Craig, 1984, 374). Though a number of veto resolutions have been introduced in foreign affairs, none has ever been passed.

Table 3.1 Trends in the Policy Uses of the Legislative Veto

| Policy Area | % of All Veto Provisions | 1920-1930s | 1940s | 1950s | 1960s | 1970-1976 |
|---|---|---|---|---|---|---|
| Agriculture & Forestry | 2.9 | ---- | ---- | 3.1 | 1.7 | 3.8 |
| Atomic Energy | 2.6 | ---- | 5.9 | 9.1 | 1.7 | 1.3 |
| Education & Research | 6.2 | ---- | ---- | ---- | ---- | 10.7 |
| Foreign Affairs | 10.2 | ---- | ---- | 3.1 | 5.1 | 15.1 |
| General Govt. & Misc. | 11.3 | 83.4 | 17.6 | 18.2 | 11.8 | 6.2 |
| Immigration | 2.2 | ---- | 17.6 | 9.1 | ---- | ---- |
| Interior Affairs & Resource Development | 15.3 | 16.6 | 5.9 | ---- | 6.8 | 22.6 |
| Military Construction & Real Property | 12.8 | ---- | 29.5 | 12.1 | 8.5 | 13.2 |
| Military Service & National Defense | 5.8 | ---- | 17.6 | 18.2 | 1.7 | 3.8 |
| NASA | 11.7 | ---- | ---- | 5.9 | 28.8 | 8.2 |
| Public Works & Transportation | 16.1 | ---- | 5.9 | 21.2 | 32.2 | 10.7 |
| Social Welfare & Labor | 2.9 | ---- | ---- | ---- | 1.7 | 4.4 |
| Total | 100% | 100% | 100% | 100% | 100% | 100% |
| N | 274 | 6 | 17 | 33 | 59 | 159 |

Source: Joseph Cooper and Patricia Hurley, "The Legislative Veto: A Policy Analysis" *Congress & the Presidency* Vol. 10, No 1, 1983 (Spring), 1-24. (Reprinted by permission)

Three principal reasons account for the differential use of legislative vetoes in domestic and foreign policy. First, Congress is more confident in domestic policy, seeing itself as the president's co-equal when it comes to policy formulation. The legislature is thus more likely to oppose the executive over policy substance and more likely to follow through when policy disagreements cannot be resolved through consultation. Second, much domestic policy is made at the agency level. Unlike foreign policy, committees and subcommittees are unlikely to come into direct confrontation with the president himself. Thwarting the plans of an unelected agency administrator is considerably less risky than thwarting the president himself. Third, organized interests are more likely to bring pressure to bear on committee members concerning regulation by an executive agency. Though there are also interest groups pressuring congressional members over foreign policy, the president is clearly the dominant force in this arena. Foreign policy is thus less susceptible to the iron triangles characteristic of much of domestic policy.

Scholars have therefore focussed their attention on domestic politics to ascertain the impact of *Chadha*. Gilmour and Craig's thinking on the subject reflects a common misperception that *Chadha* would have little effect in foreign policy. They wrote:

> With regard to the two-house arms sales veto, for example...replacing this veto with either joint resolutions of disapproval or nonbinding concurrent resolutions might appear to weaken congressional ability to achieve even these limited goals....However, the manner in which Congress actually used its arms sales veto power mitigates these concerns. Congress never exercised the concurrent veto to reject an arms sale and in those instances when the veto was used to initiate negotiations, the president would very likely have made concessions anyway, given the determined attitude of Congress....Since there is mutual advantage to the negotiations, Congress is in a strong position to bargain for a gentleman's agreement obliging the president to debate the issues and to respect a concurrent resolution of disapproval. A relationship built on such cooperation and mutual advantage is far more likely to produce positive results than the adversarial relationship inherent in the design of the veto process (Gilmour and Craig, 1984, 384).

Though their argument is appealing in its optimism, a close analysis of arms sales to the Middle East (Chapter 5) reveals that such optimism is misplaced. In fact, the effect which *Chadha* has had on interbranch relations has been precisely the opposite of their predictions. The argument of this work is that despite the fact that the legislative veto was never exercised in foreign policy, on certain issues its presence did have an impact on congressional-executive relations. Moreover, the alternatives to which Congress could turn for policy influence have made more difference than is commonly supposed.

## Arguments for and Against the Legislative Veto

The legislative veto has always been suspect on its adherence to constitutional lawmaking procedures. Article I Section 7 of the Constitution lays out the procedure by which legislation is to be enacted, requiring passage by the House of Representatives and the Senate, followed by presentation to the president for signature or veto. It further provides for the overriding of presidential veto by two-thirds of both houses of Congress. Critics argue that the legislative veto does not follow the legislating process outlined in the Constitution, and is consequently invalid.

Proponents of the legislative veto counter that since the authority under consideration is delegated to Congress by the Constitution in the first place, that Congress is entitled to determine the conditions under which it, in turn, delegates the authority to the executive. Programs, rules or initiatives taken under the delegated authority, therefore, are not subject to the same requirements of the lawmaking process.

These contrasting views provided the basis of argument for the *Chadha* case before the Supreme Court. They were not, however, the only points of debate concerning the legislative veto.

In addition to the constitutional questions surrounding the legislative veto, arguments have been raised concerning the impact which the mechanism had on the policy process. In a favorable light, the legislative veto was hailed as a useful accommodation to the complexities of modern government, a counterbalance to unchecked executive agencies or imperial presidents, and a means of decreasing congressional obstructionism in policy making. Proponents and critics alike agree that in cases of fundamental policy disagreement the legislative veto was effective in compelling consultation and compromise with the executive branch. In the absence of the congressional veto threat such comity would not have been forthcoming (Bruff and Gellhorn, 1977; Cooper and Hurley, 1983; Gilmour and Craig, 1984; Fisher, 1987).

But not all observers saw the legislative veto in a favorable light. Opponents argued that the congressional veto caused unnecessary delays in agency rulemaking and policy implementation (Bruff and Gellhorn, 1977; Gilmour, 1982; Craig, 1983). Waiting periods, whether they resulted in an actual veto or not, created unnecessary obstruction and in some instances did critical damage to the policy under consideration. Bruff and Gellhorn cite the case in which a congressional recess prior to the end of a waiting period resulted in the defeat of campaign finance rules put forward by the Federal Election Commission (Bruff and Gellhorn, 1977, 1408). But even Bruff and Gellhorn recognize that this result was more political than statutory, and cite in the same piece instances when a short waiting period has worked to the advantage of the agency, particularly when the rules under consideration were highly technical in nature.

Critics further charged that the legislative veto undermined expertise in policy by removing rulemaking from the agencies which have specialized knowledge of an issue and giving it to politicians who tend to be jacks-of-all-trades (Bruff and Gellhorn, 1977; Gilmour 1982). This charge was countered, however, by pointing to increased staff and informational resources which Congress gained in the 1970s. The rise of subcommittee policy making, it was argued, had put Congress on a competitive level in expertise, and had the added advantage of infusing a different point of view into deliberations. Contrary to critics' charges, policy deliberations were likely to include a greater number of educated opinions rather then fewer.

Perhaps the most damning criticism of the legislative veto, however, was the charge that it gave undue influence to special interest groups who were able to pressure congressional committees for preferential treatment (Bruff and Gellhorn, 1977; Ethridge, 1984). Critics cited, among other cases, Congress' repeal of Federal Trade Commission rules requiring used car dealers to inform customers of any known defects in the cars they sold (the "lemon law"). Though consumer groups successfully battled the veto in court, the case was held up as a prime example of congressional vulnerability to special interests (Gilmour and Craig, 1984). In addition, critics argued that the subsystem governments, "iron triangles," among congressional committees, special interests and the executive agencies which regulate them, benefitted from legislative vetoes since they did not entail specific, restrictive language concerning regulation. By definition, the congressional veto provision prevented Congress from having to write strict guidelines for agency rulemaking, as legislators reserved the option of nullifying any rules written by the agency staff. Thus, they left the work to the administrators. Opponents of the legislative veto argue that this flexibility allowed organized interests to take an inordinate role in the rulemaking process. Since much of the influence was behind-the-scenes, moreover, it was difficult to control or monitor (Schaefer and Thurber, 1980).

But defenders of the legislative veto countered that, in fact, regulatory agency rules was only one of several policy areas subject to the provisions, and that much of this legislation was quite detailed. Cooper and Hurley dismiss the premise that the legislative veto *necessarily* fortified governmental subsystems or that iron triangles benefited from the flexibility afforded by vague language. They argue:

> What is frequently true in non-rulemaking areas is invariably true in rulemaking areas: the veto is a symptom of discord or conflict between the legislative and executive branches of government....If relations between congressional committees and federal departments and agencies were as cozy as Schaefer and Thurber suggest, no veto provisions would be necessary. Whether vague or specific, a mutually satisfying position would be reached and written into legislation, and later congressional review of administrative actions could be handled informally in the classic cozy triangle fashion....In short, as past and continuing efforts to subject administrative rules to veto control indicate, use of the device is often a sign of dissatisfaction and lack of trust in administrators, not confidence in shared concerns (Cooper and Hurley, 1984, 15).

But even defenders of the veto conceded that the mechanism did play an important role in "pork-barrel politics" (Dodd and Schott, 1979). Given the very nature of congressional politics, one wonders whether the legislative veto could be indicted as a cause of pork or merely served as a convenient facilitator. It is clear that constituent pressure played a primary role in the legislature's use (or threatened use) of the legislative veto. Yet it would be quite a stretch to contend that pork-barrel politics has been significantly diminished by the veto's loss.

Thus the battle stood at the beginning of the 1980s. The pervasiveness of the legislative veto and its potential effects on the relationship between the political branches of government made it a source of contention on both constitutional and policy grounds. Where one stood often revealed a bias toward one or the other of the branches. Indeed, some argued that the legislative veto gave life to a *fourth* branch by delegating only loosely checked power to administrative agencies. However one came down, there was no denying that the legislative veto was an increasingly powerful weapon in Congress' policy-influencing arsenal.

### The *Chadha* Decision

Courts have not always taken a negative view of the legislative veto. In 1976 the legislative veto was challenged in a domestic case concerning the Federal Election Campaign Act as amended in 1974. The amendment greatly expanded the Federal Election Commission's (FEC) powers, yet allowed for congressional nullification of its actions via one-house veto.

The FEC challenged the legislative veto provision as unconstitutional. Ruling on the case, *Buckley v. Valeo* (424 U.S. I [1976]), Justice White argued that "In the light of modern reality, the provision for congressional disapproval of agency regulations does not appear to transgress the constitutional design...."(Pp. 284-286).

When the case was appealed in the U.S. Court of Appeals, however, Judge MacKinnon disagreed, arguing that "the one-house veto...is a completely different method of accomplishing a legislative result by a congressional procedure *not* authorized by the Constitution." He further argued that  the legislative veto "clearly violates the constitutional requirement that legislation should be passed by both houses and be signed by the president" (559 F. 2d 681 n. 4, 683-684; see Schwartz, 1981, 87).  The case was dismissed on grounds of "standing and ripeness," however, and does not constitute a precedent (*Clark v. Valeo*, 559 Fed. 2d 642 [D.C. Cir. 1977]).

Though the courts had ruled in a number of instances on issues related to the legislative veto, no ruling was ever broadly applicable to the mechanism in general. Consequently, debates over the validity of the legislative veto continued.

The case which finally brought the Supreme Court to rule on the constitutionality of the legislative veto centered on an immigration case. (For an indepth account of the *Chadha* case see Craig, 1988). For reasons which are not entirely clear, Congress overruled an INS decision to allow a number of applicants permission to immigrate.  One of those denied, surname Chadha, brought the case to court.  Chadha's lawyers argued that the congressional action was unconstitutional since the authority to grant or deny permission to immigrate had been delegated to the executive branch.  The question then was: Did Congress have the right to retain veto power over delegated authority?

A divided Court ultimately ruled in *Immigration and Naturalization Service v. Chadha (1983)* that the one-house veto  was an inappropriate alteration of the lawmaking process.  (The two-house form was ruled unconstitutional two weeks later.[5])  The ruling was based on two fundamental points:  1) the legislative veto circumvents the bicameral requirement for legislating; and 2) it violates the "presentment clause" which requires legislation to be presented to the president before it is enacted into law.

Chief Justice Burger's opinion in the case reveals an awareness by the Court of the value which the legislative veto can have in reaching settlements between the legislative and executive branches on issues under dispute, but ultimately finds in favor of a strict reading of bicameralism and the presentment clause in the Constitution.

The choices we discern as having been made in the Constitutional Convention impose burdens on governmental processes that often seem clumsy, inefficient, even unworkable, but those hard choices were consciously made by men who had lived under a form of government that permitted arbitrary governmental acts to go unchecked. There is no support in the Constitution or decisions of this Court for the proposition that the cumbersome delays often encountered in complying with explicit Constitutional standards may be avoided, either by the Congress or by the president....With all the obvious flaws of delay, untidiness and potential for abuse, we have not yet found a better way to preserve freedom than by making the exercise of power subject to the carefully crafted restraints spelled out in the Constitution....The legislative steps outlined in Article I are not empty formalities; they were designed to assure that both Houses of Congress and the president participate in the exercise of lawmaking authority....To allow Congress to evade the strictures of the Constitution and in effect enact executive proposals into law by mere silence cannot be squared with Article I (103 S. Ct. 2764 [1983]).

The dissenting opinion by Justice White illustrates the divisiveness of the debate, even within the Court itself:

If the effective functioning of a complex modern government requires the delegation of vast authority which, by virtue of its breadth, is legislative or "quasi-legislative" in character, I cannot accept that Article I--which is, after all, the source of the non-delegation doctrine--should forbid Congress from qualifying that grant with a legislative veto....The legislative veto device here--and in many other settings--is far from an instance of legislative tyranny over the executive. It is a necessary check on the unavoidably expanding power of the agencies, both executive and independent, as they engage in exercising authority delegated by Congress (103 S.Ct. 2792,2811 [1983]).

Since the *Chadha* ruling, scholars have likewise staked positions on opposing sides of the question. Opponents argue in favor of the ruling on the grounds that the legislative veto evades the presentment clause of the Constitution (Tower, 1981), that the veto was ineffective as well as unconstitutional (Gilmour and Craig, 1984; Craig 1983 and 1988) or that Congress' use of the mechanism only enhanced its ability to "dispose," making it more obstructionist than ever (Sundquist, 1976, 1984).

Supporters of the legislative veto, on the other hand, criticize the *Chadha* ruling as undermining the legitimate powers of Congress in a system of checks and balances. Referring to foreign policy, Schwartz maintains, that [the legislative veto] has been asserted over... foreign assistance and trade, which fall directly within the congressional constitutional sphere. Where the legislative veto has been used to curb the president's war powers, a strong case can be made that Congress acted in response to executive abuses that, if unchecked, would have fundamentally shifted the constitutional center of gravity (Schwartz, 1981, 98).

To some observers the very fact that the Supreme Court has ruled on the issue of the legislative veto is inappropriate. "The federal judiciary should not decide constitutional questions concerning the respective powers of Congress and the president vis-a-vis one another" argues the Dean of the U.C. Berkeley Law School:

Rather, the ultimate constitutional issues of whether executive action (or inaction) violates the prerogatives of Congress or whether legislative action (or inaction) transgresses the realm of the president should be held to be nonjusticiable, their final resolution to be remitted to the interplay of the national political process (Choper, 1980, 263).

In a similar vein, legal scholar H.H. Koh argues,

Read broadly, *Chadha* and its progeny sketch a formalistic theory of separation of powers, which rests on four basic premises: first, that the constitutional powers are functionally definable as inherently executive, judicial or legislative in nature; second that the Constitution allocates certain powers exclusively to the executive branch, thereby denying them to the other two branches; third, that Congress has limited constitutional discretion to regulate executive action by means other than formal legislation; and fourth, that these separation of powers concerns requires that specific constitutional provisions--such as the appointments or presentment clauses--be construed to invalidate even those legislative control devices that plainly promote administrative efficiency or political compromise (Koh, 1988).

Relatively little legal action has been taken by either side to challenge the *Chadha* decision. One exception was the 1986 *Alaska Airlines v. Brock* case in which the airline industry challenged legislative veto provisions in the Airline Deregulation Act of 1978 (PL 95-504). The Supreme Court ruled that legislative veto provisions do not necessarily invalidate laws in which they are found unless it can be determined that the veto provision was the primary basis for Congress' decision to delegate a given authority. Justice Blackmun wrote for the Court,

In considering this question in the context of a legislative veto, it is necessary to recognize that the absence of the veto necessarily alters the balance of powers between the legislative and executive branches of the federal government. Thus, it is not only appropriate to evaluate the importance of the veto in the original legislative bargain, but also to consider the nature of the delegated authority that Congress made subject to a veto (*CQ Almanac*, 1978, 41).

The implication of this decision is that objections to laws which contain legislative vetoes will have to be judged on a case by case basis.

In several issue areas, particularly domestic and regulatory issues, Congress and the executive have chosen not to legally contest individual laws. They have often turned to informal arrangements to achieve similar accommodations to those under the legislative veto. In such issue areas, where both parties have generally found mutual satisfaction with the legislative veto, an informal version of the committee veto still thrives (Fisher, 1989). As Frederick Kaiser of the Congressional Research Service has noted, executive agencies prefer an informal version of the legislative veto to the prospect of losing powers delegated by Congress. "Otherwise, they would lose a great amount of agency discretion" (*CQ Almanac*, 1986, 52).

On issues of foreign policy, however, the accommodation has not been so amicable. While much domestic legislation remains on the books with the legislative veto, critical pieces of foreign policy legislation have been formally amended to replace concurrent resolutions with joint resolutions of disapproval. The jealous territoriality which pervades foreign policy has not been conducive to such informal arrangements. As illustrated by the case studies (particularly arms sales to the Middle East, Chapter 5) in some instances this formal means of conforming to *Chadha* has built conflict into the structure of congressional-executive interaction. As Sen. Carl Levin (D-Mich), a leading advocate of the legislative veto has said, "*Chadha* didn't lessen the need for clearly stated arrangements of shared power between the executive and legislative branches on certain issues. It only significantly reduced our options for crafting those agreements" (*CQ Almanac*, 1986, 52).

## Alternatives to the Legislative Veto

By ruling the legislative veto unconstitutional, the Supreme Court forced Congress to choose between relinquishing its gains in foreign policy codetermination or searching for alternatives which would allow it to maintain some measure of control. It chose the latter. At the time of the ruling several observers predicted that the loss of the legislative veto would not have a significant impact upon congressional-executive relations in foreign policy. Several alternatives were available, they argued, many of which would serve the same purpose but not raise questions of constitutionality (Cooper, 1985; Fisher, 1985; Gilmour and Craig, 1984). Among the likely alternatives were: 1) restrictions on appropriations (using the power of the purse); 2) direct counter-legislation which would nullify a given initiative (subject to presidential veto); 3) "report-and-wait" provisions allowing Congress time to enact a counteracting law; 4) a joint resolution of disapproval; or 5) a joint resolution of approval.

The first of these alternatives, appropriations restrictions, is perhaps the least flexible of the alternatives. While the president may veto the legislation package in which the restriction exists, Congress is well known for its ability to couch such controversial elements in "must pass" bills, bills which include other elements of critical importance to the president. Furthermore, appropriations restrictions are likely to lead to *more* rather than less micromanagement of foreign policy as members are required to cite specific restrictions on specific programs.

Clearly the most controversy-laden of the alternatives is that of direct counter-legislation. Not only does this option ensure a highly publicized and often protracted battle but it undermines the president's credibility abroad. The ability of foreign nations to rely on the president's agreements is critical to successful foreign policy. Counter-legislation negating a presidential program (if indeed it could survive the inevitable presidential veto and battle to override) would irreparably undercut international confidence in agreements with the United States.

The joint resolutions of approval and disapproval amount to "shifting the burden" (Fisher, 1987). In place of the concurrent resolution, which is not subject to presidential veto, the court ruled that executive initiatives could only be killed through a *joint* resolution which *is* subject to presidential veto. With the joint resolution of approval the president's initiative will not become law unless proponents can organize the required majority of each house to approve the measure. Thus the burden is on the president and his supporters to ensure success. With the joint resolution of disapproval the shoe is on the other foot. The law *will* be enacted unless opponents of the measure can muster sufficient majorities in both houses to disapprove. But the battle does not end there. Should both houses disapprove a proposal the bill then goes back to the president who can veto the disapproval. Congress is then faced with the need to override the veto in order to kill the initiative.

As will be illustrated in the case studies, restrictions on appropriations and the joint resolution of disapproval have proven the most common means by which Congress has sought to maintain its codeterminative position in foreign policy. Further it will be shown that these alternatives have led to a considerably greater degree of inflexibility and conflict than was evident during the use of the legislative veto.

Whether one agrees or disagrees with the philosophy of the legislative veto, it is impossible to deny that its loss has had a significant effect on the relationship between the executive and legislative branches. It was a tool of moderation; at first symbolic of comity between the branches, later a vehicle to restrain an imperious executive without totally rescinding the delegations of authority which allowed for effective governance. It was a traffic citation rather than imprisonment. A warning meant to induce compliance but with enough potential clout to be taken seriously. Though alternative means were available to Congress in the drive to reassert its power, none held quite the same potential for mutual benefit. None was likely to achieve quite the same political accommodation as the legislative veto.

The mechanism of the legislative veto provided both the sense of control critical to congressional compromise and the flexibility essential to presidential compromise. Congress was able to present itself as a partner in the decision making process while still able to cede to the president considerable leeway in his initiatives. The veto "provided a means of securing majority support in highly decisive and politicized policy areas without imposing unbearable political costs on individual members or ceding ultimate control" (Cooper and Hurley, 1983).

It created a means "to expedite Congressional agreement--or at least the appearance of agreement--on important and highly visible policy issues where no genuine consensus exist(ed)" (Gilmour and Craig, 1984).

# 4

## The Irony of Reform:
## A Theoretical Framework

Although a multitude of legislative veto provisions were enacted, the legislative veto has never been used to kill a presidential initiative in foreign affairs (Schick, 1980; Franck and Weisband, 1979; Gilmour and Craig, 1984). The threat of its use, however, has been a fundamental force in compelling executive cooperation and consultation with Congress.

Rather than presenting policy as *fait accompli* to Congress, the president recognized the necessity of consultation for the ultimate success of his programs. Though compliance with congressional restrictions was often grudging and negotiations rocky at times, by the early 1980s Congress and the president had come to accept the need to manage conflict and come to a workable relationship. The real virtue of the legislative veto

> is that it permits two essential yet conflicting needs of the modern democratic state, executive leadership and legislative control, to be reconciled and mutually satisfied....In a variety of policy areas the veto provides the only or the best means of maintaining the exacting balance between consent and action that the Constitution intends and upon which the continued viability of our republic depends (Cooper, 1985, 379).

Optimistically, Franck and Weisband concluded, "what was once resisted as dangerous congressional trespassing on executive prerogatives has now been recognized as a healthy reform of U.S. policy as well as of executive-congressional relations" (Franck and Weisband, 1979, 97). It may be more accurate to envision the executive reluctantly taking the medicine rather than coming to some newfound revelation about the

43

desirability of the reform. In any event Congress was a player and compromise was the name of the game.

This chapter focusses on the theoretical framework for determining under what circumstances the *Chadha* decision will have an impact on congressional-executive relations in foreign policy. The primary goal is to determine what factors or variables promote conflict between the branches. The greater the conflict potential in a given issue area, the greater the impact of *Chadha*. In circumstances of conflict between the branches, the legislative veto was a unique tool to forge an accommodation, a means to resolve (or at least mitigate) conflict in a behind-the-scenes manner. Without the legislative veto the means Congress has been forced to adopt in the effort to assert its views in foreign policy have resulted in higher profile conflict between the branches.

But because all issues in foreign policy are not equally conflictive, the impact of *Chadha* varies by issue type. So what are the characteristics which lead to greater or lesser degrees of conflict? The answer is the subject of this chapter.


## When Congress Gets Involved

The underlying goal of this study is to evaluate the impact of the *Chadha* decision on congressional-executive relations in the making of American foreign policy. It is argued that in some instances *Chadha* has resulted in greater interbranch conflict while in others it has had little or no impact. But the impact of the *Chadha* decision itself is dependent upon the nature of the issue, specifically: 1) the likelihood of congressional involvement in the issue; 2) presidential claims of independent authority to determine policy on the issue; and 3) congressional will to assert itself. These variables determine the degree to which disagreement between the branches is likely to lead to conflict. The legislative veto, it is argued, was a mechanism through which Congress could compel at least consultation and at times compromise from the executive branch. In turn, these conflicts could be resolved (at least temporarily) in a more circumspect, less overt manner. The loss of the legislative veto, has forced Congress to adopt alternative means to assert its prerogatives in foreign policy decisionmaking-- alternatives which result in higher profile, more overt conflict between the branches. The *Chadha* decision, then, serves as an *intervening variable* between those variables which lead to the *likelihood* of conflict and the ensuing *intensity* of conflict.

The impact of *Chadha* becomes relevant when the preconditions for potential conflict between the branches are satisfied. That is, when Congress asserts itself, there is policy disagreement, and when Congress has the will to act. It is at this point that the legislative veto served to diffuse conflict through consultation and compromise. In the absence of the legislative veto conflict is more overt.

If any of the preconditions are not met, conflict does not ensue. In the case studies to follow, for example, we see that in war powers legislators do not have the electoral motivation to oppose the president. In addition, Congress as an institution lacks the will to take on responsibility for policy in crisis situations and has trouble building coalitions strong enough for effective opposition to executive action. Thus the potential for conflict is averted early on. The legislative veto, therefore, never becomes a serious option for action.

In order to adequately evaluate *Chadha's* impact, then, it is first necessary to take a closer look at the factors which determine the level of interbranch conflict in foreign policy. This section will lay out the theoretical argument which serves as the basis of the study. Later chapters will present case studies which illustrate that differing issue types hold differing potential for executive-legislative conflict, and consequently have been affected differently by the loss of the legislative veto.

### Dependent Variable

The dependent variable in this study is the *intensity* of conflict between the executive and legislative branches of government. Measuring the intensity of conflict between Congress and the executive presents a variety of problems, both conceptual and methodological. In essence, 'How do you know conflict when you see it?' and, more importantly, 'How do you measure it?'

There are few precedents in the literature on congressional-executive relations in foreign policy to guide quantitative research. Though interbranch conflict over foreign policy is a well reviewed topic, the overwhelming method of analysis has been qualitative case studies. The work of Dahl (1950) and Robinson (1962, 1967) are exceptions to the rule. Dahl does engage in some quantitative analysis in his classic work *Congress and Foreign Policy*, but focusses primarily upon interparty cleavages rather than inter-institutional ones.

Robinson's quantitative analysis in *Congress and Foreign Policy-Making* comes closer to the objective. He presents correlations between the degree to which members of Congress express satisfaction with the policy making process and their degree of satisfaction with policy outcomes (Robinson, 1967, 166). This analysis is cross-sectional, however, and does not really strike at the heart of interbranch conflict on an issue over time.

A decade later, Fenno included some aggregate data to complement his interviews of members on the Foreign Affairs Committee in *Congressmen in Committees* (Fenno, 1973). Still, his focus concerned member goals and not specifically interbranch conflict over time.

As Deering lamented in 1983, "it is disappointing to note, despite dramatic changes in Congress...little behavioral research has focussed on Congress and foreign policy" (Deering, 1983, 243).

In this study conflict intensity is measured by the number of bills and resolutions introduced in Congress to kill or limit an executive policy or proposal. In the aftermath of the *Chadha* decision Congress has been forced to use more direct counter-legislation, appropriations limitations and resolutions of disapproval in order to compel consultation or compromise and influence policy outcomes on issues of contention between the executive and legislative branches. Not only is the introduction of such legislation a public gesture, but the ensuing debate and vote bring public attention to the issue and, more importantly, to disagreements with executive policy.

This measure cuts to the heart of the argument presented here. If, as I have argued, conflict has increased in those issue areas in which members of Congress have sufficient electoral and legislative incentive to confront the president, we should see a concomitant increase in the number of bills and resolutions introduced since 1983. For those issues in which the *Chadha* decision is argued to have had little or no effect no such trend should be apparent.

The number of bills and resolutions introduced in opposition to executive policy in each issue area has been catalogued from 1977-1989.[6] To do this a number of complementary sources have been used: the Congressional Research Service *Digest of General Public Bills and Resolutions*, committee calendars, and the *Congressional Record Index*.

Since the intention is to measure conflict between members of Congress and the president, bills and resolutions which were introduced at the request of the executive, supported his legislative agenda, or increased his policy making latitude and flexibility were excluded. Thus only those bills and resolution which limited or conflicted with the executive position on the issue were included.

Note that this measure includes bills and resolutions *introduced* rather than bills and resolutions *passed*. Recall that much of the aim of contentious legislative activity is to compel compromise on a given policy issue rather than to dominate policy outcomes per se. Congress wants influence but not necessarily responsibility. Looking at the introduction of restrictive legislation, therefore, gives us a picture which includes the threats and grandstanding which often play a critical role in Congress' ability to force compromise in a variety of policy areas.

It is also important to distinguish that the dependent variable is not merely the existence or absence of conflict, but its relative intensity over time. Indeed, the very existence of conflict is a necessary precondition to determine the impact of the *Chadha* decision. The argument is that given the existence of congressional-executive conflict in a foreign policy issue, the legislative veto allowed for reconcilliation in a behind-the-scenes, relatively unobtrusive manner. In the absence of the legislative veto, foreign policy conflicts are debated and reconciled in a much more high profile, public manner.

## Independent Variables

The independent variables which determine the potential for conflict are: congressional assertiveness, presidential claims of authority, and congressional will to oppose the president on a given issue.

Congressional assertiveness can further be broken down into the *institutional* and *electoral* motivations which legislators have to become involved in a particular issue of foreign policy. These two factors are distinct and necessary for congressional assertiveness. Congressional assertiveness, in turn, is a necessary but not sufficient condition for conflict. Without congressional assertiveness the executive branch is free to conduct foreign policy in the manner in which it sees fit. While there may be some rhetorical jousting between the branches, without congressional assertion conflict is negligible.

*Institutional Motives.* The decade of the 1970s was a clear demonstration of the institutional stake which Congress has in becoming a partner in foreign policy. The institutional motives discussed in this study refer to the constitutional powers delegated to Congress to declare war, raise and support armies, regulate foreign commerce, issue letters of marque and reprisal as well as the Senate's authority to consent to treaty ratification and confirm ambassadors. These provide the foundations of the institutional role in foreign affairs.

The frustrations which had been building over the executive handling of foreign policy in the 1960s and early 1970s contributed to the momentum building behind the drive for congressional reassertion.

Though Congress was equally to blame for the dominant position which the executive held in the making of postwar U.S. foreign policy, a significant number of members came to see the pendulum as having swung too far, eclipsing the role of Congress to an inordinate degree. Presidents were able to take an "imperial" position in foreign policy because the congressional check on his actions had become ineffectual. The role that Congress, *as a governmental institution*, played in foreign policy decision making needed to be strengthened.

The perception among members that the institution could and *should* be strengthened is critical to an understanding of the current relationship between Congress and the executive. Contrast the congressional reaction to American involvement in the Korean War with American involvement in the Vietnam War (McCormick and Wittkopf, 1990). While there was considerable protest over Truman's cavalier handling of the introduction of American forces with only cursory attention paid to Congress, there was not a movement to change the *institutional* balance of power. This period was marked by an unprecedented international role for the United States in world politics, a unity of purpose in American foreign policy (containment of communism), and a strong belief in bipartisanship (thanks to a significant degree to Senator Arthur Vandenberg). Presidential direction of foreign policy was, therefore, not only practical but desirable; hence congressional willingness to delegate authority. Thus, while there was disagreement concerning certain presidential actions *within* this overall structure of congressional-executive relations, there was no drive to change the structure itself. The institutional role of Congress was generally believed to be appropriate.

In the 1970s, by contrast, consensus over the goals and methods of American foreign policy had weakened, and with it the complacency of legislators in their institutional role. As views concerning the design of American policy diverged concerns arose over the ability of Congress to assert its own policy preferences or check those of the president. Conflict over American involvement in Vietnam, therefore, was not limited to mere policy disagreement but to a reevaluation of the entire structure of congressional-executive relations. But 25 years of congressional acquiescence and executive dominance had left Congress both psychologically and practically out of touch with the role which it was constitutionally delegated. Thus, regaining the lost stature of *Congress as an institution* became a significant motive affecting members' considerations in foreign policy. Legislators' awareness of their role as members of the institution instills in each individual an institutional motivation to be part of a strong Congress. Legislators, therefore, will be motivated to become involved in those foreign policy issues in which

Congress has a constitutionally delegated role and which are perceived to affect its institutional standing vis-a-vis the executive.

*Electoral Motives.* In foreign policy, as in domestic policy, the institutional role must coexist (sometimes conflict) with the electoral role of each member as a power broker within the institution and as a re-election-minded politician vulnerable to constituency pressures.

The electoral motives that inspire a legislator to become involved in a given foreign policy issue may well be part of an attempt to become a "power entrepreneur" or "policy entrepreneur" (Dodd, 1977) staking out a position for themselves within the congressional power structure. A position on one of the committees which deal with foreign policy is the most direct point of access to consideration of such issues, though with increasing frequency members have adopted individual foreign policy issues regardless of their committee assignments (Sinclair, 1989; Smith, 1989).

Few would argue with the premise that the overriding motive of individual members of Congress is re-election (Mayhew, 1974). The pursuit of this goal is precisely what makes Congress the governmental institution most accessible to the public, particularly organized groups. The prospect of electoral capital provides strong motivation to become involved in a given foreign policy issue of importance to a member's constituents.

The factors which affect the prospect of electoral gain, and hence the motivation for involvement in a given foreign policy issue include: intensity of interest group pressure in one's constituency; salience of the issue to the public; and information and understanding available to members about the issue. These appear in varying combinations, depending upon the issue at hand. All issues are affected by systematic variations in electoral motivations. This variation, along with institutional motives, determines the degree of congressional assertion in a foreign policy issue.

As will be seen in the case studies to follow, constituency pressure is arguably the most powerful motivator of individual members. This is the factor with the most direct electoral connection.

There are a number of foreign policy issues which are of relatively little salience in the state or district and on which a legislator has considerable latitude to develop a policy stance (Kingdon, 1973; Franck and Weisband, 1979). On these issues the member will, of course, be concerned about how his/her issue stance will "play in Peoria" but will direct primary attention to substantive policy considerations.

In order to understand the factors which determine whether or not Congress will prove assertive or acquiescent in a given issue area of foreign policy, one must understand the relative power of the institutional versus electoral motivations in the context of that issue. At times these may coincide. At other times they will conflict. Of the two, electoral motivations appear to be the more powerful. Clearly legislators will not act in the absence of institutional motivations, but when institutional and electoral motives conflict the electoral motives are generally more powerful. Given the increasingly individualistic nature of Congress over the past two decades this is not particularly surprising. The primary motive of any legislator is to remain a legislator. Otherwise, institutional motivations are moot. Thus, while institutional motives are of real importance in analyzing congressional assertion, they must be considered secondary to electoral motives.

Congressional assertion is a necessary but not sufficient condition for conflict between the branches over foreign policy. Not every issue on which Congress asserts its view becomes conflictive. There are a number of issues on which Congress and the president see eye-to-eye, where mutual partisan consent keeps the issue from causing friction.

In order for an issue to be conflictive there must, of course, be policy disagreement. But the story does not end there. The potential for policy disagreement to become interbranch conflict is determined by: 1) presidential claims of authority over the issue; and 2) congressional will to act in opposition to the president.

*Presidential Claims of Authority.* Another factor which determines the potential for interbranch conflict comes from the executive side. That is the degree to which the president views the issue as within the domain of the executive; the executive claim to determine policy based upon inherent powers, independent of approval from Congress.

In the postwar period presidents have increasingly come to view practically all areas of foreign policy as executive territory, a view aided, no doubt by the *Curtiss-Wright* case. Congressional willingness to follow the president's lead in forging the United States' new role as a superpower has fortified this view, such that it has become commonplace to look to the executive for definition in international relations.

As a determinant of potential conflict between Congress and the executive, theoretically, the more the president claims authority in an issue area the greater the potential for conflict. The more a president sees policy making in a given issue area as an executive function the less likely he is to consult or compromise with legislators on policy substance.

Since the period under study is entirely within the postwar period, however, presidential claims of authority is not a variable in the statistical sense (i.e. that its value differs across cases), rhetoric notwithstanding. If one were to consider presidential claims as a binary variable (Yes [1], No [0]) then the values in the postwar period would be constant at 1. Were one to run this factor as an independent variable in a model of interbranch conflict, then, the results would show presidential claims of authority to be an inconsequential factor since it does not vary. A constant independent variable cannot be used to determine the source of variance in a dependent variable.

But this result would be misleading. Though presidential claims of authority do not vary in the postwar period under study, it is still an important factor in the current context surrounding congressional-executive relations in foreign policy. Presidential claims of authority have not been constant over history. In the period following the Civil War and between the two World Wars foreign policy was dominated by Congress. In the early years of the republic there was a greater balance between the institutions in the determination of foreign policy. The fact that the president now considers foreign policy to be within the executive domain is a significant factor in the discontent of Congress. It is at the heart of the institutional struggle and disagreements over the constitutional delegation of powers in foreign policy.

In the postwar period it was mutually accepted by (most) legislators and presidents that it was *functionally* appropriate to allow the executive to take the lead in foreign policy (Glennon, 1990). With its superior information gathering capabilities, hierarchical organization, and general advantages of "secrecy and dispatch," Congress was willing to cede to the president much of its constitutionally delegated role in the interests of an effective American foreign policy at a critical period in history. It was willing to do this *so long as* it could retain ultimate oversight. This was the glory of the legislative veto.

But forty years of practically unrestrained leeway have had the effect of inducing historical amnesia--presidents (and even some legislators) came to see foreign policy making as the executive's inherent right. They forgot that presidential leadership was a functional response to the dilemmas facing a new superpower. When Congress sought to reestablish an institutional balance, and regain a significant role in foreign policy, their efforts were seen as an attempt to usurp an executive function.

Presidential claims of authority across the spectrum of foreign policy issues is thus a critical factor in the current context of interbranch relations. It is the basis of executive intransigence in the face of congressional demands for policy input, and a fundamental source of potential conflict.

*Congressional Will.* In order to effectively oppose the president in foreign policy Congress must have the will to use the statutory tools at its disposal. Though each legislator must have the individual motivations (institutional and electoral) to act, congressional will is a collective attribute. A few vocal members may make an issue uncomfortable for the president, but have limited effect unless they are able to galvanize the support of a super-majority of their colleagues. To present a credible threat to executive policy the members of Congress must demonstrate resolve in their policy opposition. They must demonstrate congressional will.

In analyzing this variable, we are shifting from an individual level of analysis to a collective or group level. We are looking at Congress as an institution, the sum of its individual members. This is important to do when considering relations between the branches because Congress does have an institutional character which is distinct from individual legislators. Individual representatives do not have a constitutional role independent of their position in the institution. It is the legislature which is accorded constitutional powers, not individual members. Thus, legislators' collective action in opposition to the executive finds its substance in the institutional role which they seek to protect or to assert.

A number of elements provide the foundation for congressional will to act: presidential standing; interest group or public opinion pressure on the institution; and congressional willingness to take responsibilty for policy.

Congress is reluctant to oppose a popular president. Thus a president who enjoys broad popularity with the public also enjoys significant power to dictate policy. This is even more so in foreign policy, the postwar domain of presidents. By the same token, a president who fails to capture the imagination and confidence of the nation may also find himself the target of widespread congressional opposition. The legislature risks less by opposing a weak president than a strong one because the public is less likely to criticize Congress for taking an opposing policy stand. Charges of obstructionism are less likely to arise. Thus presidential standing is an important factor in determining congressional will to oppose the executive.

Congressional willingness to oppose the president is fortified, often catalyzed, by the public's expectation that Congress act on a given issue. In contrast to constituent pressure on an individual representative, this factor refers to a perception among the national public that action by

Congress as an institution is appropriate and necessary. If the public appears to consider an issue area to be the sole purview of the executive, as is often the case in crisis situations, then congressional action is likely to be perceived as obstructionist. If, by contrast, the public looks to Congress for action on a given issue, congressional *in*action will be perceived as a demonstration of institutional weakness or incompotence. The case of MFN trade status for China demonstrates a situation in which public expectations brought significant pressure on Congress to derail executive extension of trade benefits. The high profile of recent debates over China's trade status demonstrate the degree to which Congress is inspired to rise to meet public expectations.

An important factor mitigating *against* congressional action is the legislature's reluctance to take responsibility for policy, particularly foreign policy. Still bruised from criticism over Versailles and isolationism, Congress has been extremely wary of taking the lead role in policy formulation. Indeed, it is probably more to the point to say that Congress does not want to take the *blame* for unsuccessful policy. In an area as unpredictable and quixotic as foreign affairs, potential for failure is great. Thus, while Congress wants to ensure its role as a participant in foreign policy formulation, it is averse to take a position of leadership. Congressional inaction can be overcome, however, if public pressure is strong enough, if the president's standing is especially weak or if the policy under consideration holds substantial promise for success.

### Whither Conflict? Foreign Policy Issue Types and the Potential for Conflict

Even a cursory examination of foreign policy reveals that not all issues inspire disagreement between Congress and the executive. In a number of cases the branches agree on policy and conflict never arises. Though we have discussed the variables which determine the potential for conflict, we still lack a comprehensive framework to explain conflict and consensus in foreign policy.

This section, therefore, presents a typology of foreign policy issues which are characterized by systematic variations in congressional assertion, congressional will, policy making process and the consequent impact of *Chadha*. The case studies presented in Chapters 5 through 8 are representative of these broad issue types and illustrate in specific detail why some issue types inspire interbranch conflict while others do not.

Foreign policy issues can be divided into four broad categories: symbolic/ceremonial; crisis; strategic; and intermestic. Strategic issues can further be subdivided into salient and non-salient issues. Each of these issue types is distinguished by characteristics which make it more or less prone to interbranch conflict. In turn, each has been impacted by the *Chadha* decision in a manner proportionate to its potential for conflict.

Table 4.1 presents a typology of foreign policy issue areas, the characteristics which determine the potential for conflict in each type, the effect which the *Chadha* decision has had, and an example of each issue type. Though representative case studies will be examined in detail, it is useful at this point to look more closely at the array of issue types. One of the pervasive problems in the study of American foreign policy has been the tendency to limit analysis to one or a few case studies, often unique in character, without a comprehensive view toward a more generalizable theoretical argument (Deering, 1983). While this study will also look at specific case studies, this typology allows us to fit the cases into a more comprehensive argument concerning the process of foreign policy making.

Taking each issue type in turn we now can evaluate the interactions of the aforementioned independent variables and their role in increasing or decreasing the potential for interbranch conflict in the process of formulating American foreign policy. In addition, we can evaluate the role which the legislative veto played in each issue type, and, given a particular level of potential conflict, come to some conclusions about the variable impact of the *Chadha* decision.

### Symbolic/Ceremonial

Symbolic/ceremonial issues include the recognition of foreign governments and the receiving of foreign dignitaries and heads of state. These functions are constitutionally delegated to the executive: ceremonial functions such as receiving ambassadors are explicitly delegated to the president in Article II Section 3 and the recognition of foreign governments is inferred from this passage. The practice of recognizing foreign governments has been further fortified by custom (Glennon, 1990). Legislators have neither an institutional nor electoral incentive to assume these functions. In turn, there is no incentive for Congress as an institution to take the lead in ceremonial or symbolic diplomatic functions. Congress has generally deferred to the president on issues of ceremonial or symbolic diplomacy. Though opinions on international relations are inevitably expressed by individual legislators, the process of policy making on this issue type has been left to the executive.

Table 4.1 - Characteristics of Foreign Policy Issue Types and the Impact of *Chadha*

| | Institutional Motives | Electoral Motives | Congr. Will | Process Prior to *Chadha* | Centrality of Legisl. Veto as Instrument of Influence | Process After *Chadha* | Effect of *Chadha* | Example |
|---|---|---|---|---|---|---|---|---|
| Diplomatic/Ceremonial | None | None | None | Deference to Executive | Not Applicable | Deference to Executive | None | Receive Foreign Heads of State |
| Crisis | High | Low | Low | Request Consultation / Support Executive | Not Central | Request Consultation / Support Executive | Little/None | War Powers |
| Strategic Non-salient | High | Low | Low to Moderate | Report and Wait / Occasional Leg. Veto Threat | Important | Weak Attempts to Modify Exec. Actions w/ Weak Legislation | Moderate to Occasional Conflict | Nuclear Non-Proliferation |
| Strategic Salient | High | High | High | Compel Consultation via Leg. Veto Threat | Central | Resolutions of Disapproval / Counter-legislation | Increase Profile of Conflict | Arms Sales To Middle East |
| Intermestic | High | High | High | Compel Consultation via Leg. Veto Threat | Central | Resolutions of Disapproval / Counter-legislation / Hearings | Increase Profile of Conflict | Most Favored Nation Trade Status |

Thus, conflict between the branches is minimal or nonexistent. Since ceremonial/symbolic diplomatic functions were not delegated to the executive by the legislature the legislative veto had no practical application. The *Chadha* decision thus had no effect in this area of policy.

## Crisis

Crisis issues necessitate quick and decisive action. It is generally argued that these are more appropriately left to the "secrecy and dispatch" of the executive branch than to the public deliberations of the legislature. Issues involving war powers are classic examples of crisis issues. (Even if the actual event itself is not inherently a crisis situation the executive generally couches debate over the event in crisis terms. Witness, for example, the debate surrounding President Reagan's order for the invasion of Grenada).

The constitutionally delegated power to declare war, coupled with the overall import of crisis issues to the national interest, gives representatives high institutional motivation to participate in policy making. This is countered, indeed generally overwhelmed, by low electoral motivation for policy participation.

In crisis issues, the rally-round-the-flag effect on public opinion and the perception that the nation's interests are at stake all contribute to legislators' personal reluctance to oppose the president. Members fear that a dissenting vote would be used against them in the next reelection campaign, thus they tend to support the president. Supporting the president is essentially a win-win stance for legislators. If the action succeeds they claim credit for having supported it. If the action fails, they blame the president but claim credit for having supported him in the interests of national unity.

The public perception that the president should be supported in times of crisis works against congressional will to act in opposition. In addition, crisis situations are rife with potential for policy failure. Congress wants to be consulted and informed on policy, but does not want to assume the responsibility (or blame) for outcomes. Thus while the legislative veto is written into legislation, there is little incentive to enforce it and take over policy making.

The process of policy making, both before and after the Court's decision, has been for Congress to demand consultation but ultimately to defer to the president. The *Chadha* decision consequently has had little effect in this area of policy.

## Strategic

Strategic issues are those which affect the relative power balance in the international system. In the post-war period in particular, members of Congress are willing to give the president a great deal of flexibility on these issues *unless* the issue is highly salient to his/her constituents.

An example of a *strategic-nonsalient* issue is nuclear nonproliferation. Though public concern over the uncontrolled spread of nuclear weapons and technology was high in the early 1970s its salience to the general public has declined considerably in the 1980s. Thus, while Congress has high institutional motivation to oversee and control the distribution of nuclear capabilities for both interstate commerce and national security reasons, legislators have low electoral motivation to expend precious time and energy on the issue.

While a group of legislators may have a strong commitment to vigilant oversight in this area, strategic issues are generally considered by the public to be the president's terrain. Lacking public pressure, even strongly committed individual legislators have difficulty inspiring their responsibility-averse colleagues to action. The congressional will necessary to oppose the executive in cases of policy disagreement is low to moderate at best.

Still, congressional consensus on the importance of strategic issues in general has been sufficient to impose report-and-wait conditions on executive action, occasionally augmented by the threatened use of the legislative veto. In spite of relatively weak resolve to use the veto, the tool was important to congressional influence in strategic policy making. In its absence Congress has made some attempts to influence executive action through legislation, but the same factors which mitigate against electoral motivation and congressional will have also resulted in weak statutory restrictions. The *Chadha* decision has thus resulted in moderate, occasional conflict over strategic-nonsalient issues.

In *strategic-salient* issues, however, constituent pressure, playing on reelection concerns, ensures congressional assertion in policy making. Legislators have high motivation, both institutional and electoral, for policy involvement.

The importance of strategic issues, particularly when coupled with public expectations of congressional action, underpins congressional will to act. In strategic-salient issues Congress was most likely to compel consultation from the executive through the legislative veto threat. Arms sales to the Middle East provides a classic example.

Since strategic foreign policy has come to be seen by post-war presidents as inherently in the executive domain, policy disagreements have the potential for considerable conflict. The impact of *Chadha* has been great in strategic-salient issues, therefore, where Congress has been unwilling to acquiesce and has been driven to adopt statutory alternatives such as counter-legislation and resolutions of disapproval which bring interbranch conflict into full public view.

## Intermestic

Intermestic issues combine both domestic policy and foreign (international) policy (Hammond, 1986). By their very nature, they involve the interests of one or more groups within legislators' constituencies and thus induce congressional assertion. The extension of most-favored-nation (MFN) trade status to foreign nations is a prime example of an intermestic issue. Institutional motivations based upon the constitutionally delegated power to regulate interstate commerce are fortified by electoral motivations to satisfy constituent pressures.

Often legislators and executives face similar interest group pressures and take a common policy stance (Pastor, 1980; Ripley and Franklin, 1984). There are, however, times when policy disagreements arise and the potential for conflict is great. This was particularly true in the debate over MFN to China after the massacres in Tienanmen Square. Executive claims of authority to use trade status as a tool of foreign policy clashed head-on with congressional will to oppose the president. Public expectations were high for congressional participation, as was Congress' confidence in its role in trade policy.

The legislative veto provided a powerful tool of influence--one which Congress had strong incentive to use. Thus, as with strategic-salient issues, the conflict surrounding intermestic issues is likely to become higher in profile as Congress is forced to adopt alternative means to influence policy.

In sum, then, when evaluating the impact of *Chadha* it is not enough to cite Congress' feeble performance in war powers as the basis for concluding that the legislative veto was useless in general. Nor is it sufficient to say that because no legislative vetoes were ever passed in foreign policy that the mechanism was ineffectual. To understand the import of the legislative veto in the formulation of American foreign policy and the relationship between the congressional and executive branches, one must appreciate the context in which the tool was of greater and lesser value. The legislative veto's practical applicability varied by issue type. As a result, the loss of the veto has had differing impacts depending on the nature of the issue under consideration.

Previous scholarship analyzing the impact of the *Chadha* decision would not have led us to expect the powerful impact which the loss of the legislative veto has had in certain areas of foreign policy. With the perspective which a decade of experience lends, we can now look back upon congressional-executive interaction in foreign policy and see that while Congress does indeed have alternatives to the legislative veto, these alternatives are not, in fact, the near substitutes which scholars had predicted (Cooper and Hurley, 1983; Cooper, 1985; Gilmour and Craig, 1984; Fisher, 1987).

Though even opponents of the legislative veto noted that the *Chadha* decision may affect arms sales to the Middle East (Gilmour and Craig, 1984) this case was singled out as a unique exception. What they failed to appreciate, however, is the underlying theoretical framework which accounts for the varying impact of *Chadha* on cases like arms sales and war powers. What this typology provides is a more comprehensive view of foreign policy and a theoretical structure to account for differences in the policy making processes among issue types. Rather than treating foreign policy making as a monolithic endeavor, this framework recognizes the nuance and variety in the array of foreign policy decisions facing policy makers. Thus, where other scholars view a case such as arms sales to the Middle East as a unique outlier in the study of the legislative veto, this work sees it as a case representative of a broad category of strategic-salient issues, each of which share characteristics which predispose them to interbranch conflict. From this perspective it is not at all surprising that the loss of the legislative veto has had significant impact on legislative-executive relations in this issue area while at the same time having little or no impact elsewhere.

## Conflict and Consensus in American Foreign Policy

Looking at the landscape of foreign policy issues it is readily apparent that some issues which appear on the surface to be very similar inspire widely differing degrees of conflict. Why, for example do arms sales to the Middle East regularly draw intense interbranch fire while arms sales to Asia do not? Why does Jewish emigration from the USSR capture the attention of powerful legislators while the flight of boatpeople from Vietnam gains only peripheral notice? Why has the nuclear capability of Pakistan or Iraq become a rallying point while Israel's nuclear capability gets a wink and a nod from both branches of the U.S. government? The answer is heavily based upon domestic politics.

Using the framework in Table 4.1 we can come to some answers to these questions. Even seemingly similar cases within the same issue category (arms sales to the Middle East vs. arms sales to South Asia, for instance) are actually representative of different issue types because of the politics surrounding them. Because arms sales to the Middle East is highly salient to a powerful lobbying organization it becomes a strategic-salient issue, while arms to India is more likely to be strategic-nonsalient. Likewise foreign aid to Turkey and Greece has been a point of considerable contention while similar aid to many African countries inspires little notice. The constituent pressure on legislators to gain favorable aid packages for Greece and Turkey (particularly from the Greek lobby demanding at least partial equity with Turkey) is not present in most African cases. Thus where one case of aid is strategic-salient, the other is strategic-nonsalient.

The point is that the politics surrounding the making of foreign policy is critical to the temper of interbranch relations. Politics vary, and so do interbranch relations. To understand the nature of foreign policy, therefore, one must look below the surface of issues and appreciate the forces motivating the participation of each branch. The framework in Table 4.1 provides a theoretical foundation for evaluating policy makers' motivations, the likelihood of conflict between and among these motivations, and the consequent impact which changes in the statutory tools available to resolve that conflict will have on the process of policy formulation.

# 5

# From Codetermination to Conflict: Arms Sales to the Middle East

The sale of arms to the Middle East is among the most controversial issues in American foreign policy. The recurring struggle pits the executive branch, trying to maintain leverage among Arab nations through arms sales, against Congress, often considered the bastion of support for Israel. The case presents a prime example of the need for effective conflict resolution in interbranch policy disagreement. It is also the case in which the loss of the legislative veto has had the most detrimental effect.

Arms sales to the Middle East is an example of a strategic-salient issue. It is strategic because the ability of individual countries in the region to acquire arms determines the balance of power in the Middle East. It is salient because of the geostrategic importance of the region and U.S. dependence upon Middle East oil. Even more importantly, however, it is salient to the powerful pro-Israeli lobby in the United States and the increasingly important Arab lobby.

As a strategic-salient issue, arms sales to the Middle East presents a high potential for congressional-executive conflict since Congress has the incentive and the will to oppose the president in cases of policy disagreement. The legislative veto was a major statutory weapon of influence, and its loss has had an ironic and detrimental impact on the policy making process in this area. The ruling in the *Chadha* case changed the structural context of congressional-executive interaction, transforming it from one of grudging yet effective cooperation into one marked by increasingly rigid and inflexible conflict.

## Determining the Potential for Conflict

An explicit look at the variables affecting the policy process of arms sales to the Middle East will better illustrate just why relations between the branches hold such high potential for conflict. In turn, it will reveal the importance of the legislative veto in resolving congressional-executive conflict and the consequent effect of the *Chadha* decision.

### *Institutional Motives for Congressional Action*

Article I Section 8 of the Constitution delegates to Congress the power to regulate commerce with foreign nations. Arms sales clearly falls within that realm. This power alone establishes an institutional motivation for congressional involvement in policy making. But beyond this explicit power, the Constitution charges Congress "to make all laws which shall be necessary and proper for carrying into execution the foregoing powers, and all other powers vested by this Constitution in the government of the United States or in any department or officer thereof." Herein lies much of the controversy--what exactly are the boundaries defined by "necessary and proper?" To Congress the phrase gives the legislature a fundamental role in any aspect of foreign policy which impacts upon its explicit powers. Thus, any U.S. actions which affect decisions concerning commerce with foreign nations are also within the congressional purview.

Congress has argued that successive administrations, particularly since Nixon, have used arms sales as a major tool of foreign policy in the Middle East (and elsewhere in the world). As such, not only does Congress have a pivotal role from the perspective of foreign commerce, but the results of the sales affect global hostilities and, potentially, U.S. involvement in war. Given the geostrategic and economic interest which the U.S. maintains in the Middle East, regional instability, born of an arms race, has strong potential for drawing an American military reaction. As Madison argued, the executive is not at liberty to create an "antecedent state of things" which leaves Congress no option but to involve the U.S. military in hostilities. Legislators must be consulted, they argue, on matters of such strategic international importance. Thus members of Congress have a strong institutional motivation to involve themselves in the formulation of policy concerning American arms sales to the Middle East.

## *Electoral Motives for Congressional Action*

The primary electoral motive catalyzing legislators' involvement in arms sales to the Middle East is the re-election motive. The strength of the pro-Israeli lobby (particularly the American-Israeli Political Action Committee, AIPAC) is notorious in pressuring legislators to protect the interests of Israel. The issue of arms sales to Israel's Arab neighbors (and enemies) is of central concern to the pro-Israeli lobby and thus serves as a measuring stick for determining representatives' solidarity with their cause. A legislator who is perceived to be hostile to Israel is almost sure to meet heavy opposition in a reelection campaign and, if the district contains a large Jewish population, faces the strong possibility of defeat.

In a related way, arms sales to the Middle East provides a powerful issue for the policy entrepreneur. As a member of a committee which deals with arms sales and a leader in introducing legislation, not only will the representative gain points for being in the forefront on the issue, but will gain leverage vis-a-vis colleagues who also face pressure from the pro-Israeli lobby. An issue of such strategic importance to U.S. interests abroad also provides impressive foreign policy credentials to the representative with presidential aspirations.

A somewhat absurd demonstration of legislators' drive to be viewed as supportive of Israeli interests was evident in the debate over the sale of missiles to Kuwait in 1988. A vociferous and highly publicized debate the year before over the sale of Maverick D missiles to Saudi Arabia had made the Maverick Ds "a sort of litmus test of those who were under pressure from Israel," according to one State Department official. Members of Congress forced a compromise, of sorts, demanding that the administration replace the dreaded Maverick D missiles with another model, Maverick Gs, in the arms sale proposal. The absurdity was that the Maverick Gs actually had greater distance capabilities and for all practical purposes posed a greater threat to Israel than did the Maverick Ds. But Maverick Ds were the ones which Israel opposed, so Maverick Ds were forced out of the agreement. As the State Department liaison to Congress recalled, "The Kuwaitis were pinching themselves to try to understand the change."

Legislators thus have high electoral motivation to become involved on issues of arms sales to the Middle East and oppose executive proposals which appear to threaten the interests of Israel. This motivation is primarily based on reelection prospects, but also on the realization of the benefits to be had by taking a leadership role in this particular policy area. Coupled with the institutional motivation, legislators' electoral motivation to participate in policy making ensures congressional assertion when it comes to arms sales to the Middle East.

## Congressional Will to Act

The strength of the national pro-Israeli lobby, and the clearly defined constitutional role for Congress in foreign commerce provide a strong foundation for the congressional will to act. In addition, the strength of the U.S. alliance with Israel and the potential instability of many of the Arab states in the Middle East make conservatism in arms sales a reasonably safe policy stance. Still, Congress does not want to take full responsibility for American foreign policy, particularly in an area as volatile as the Middle East.

Consultation and compromise is what Congress is after on the issue of arms sales to the Middle East. Because of the strong pressures on them, legislators have threatened to veto executive initiatives in order to compel cooperation from the executive. The credibility in these threats comes from the realization that Congress has the will to carry them through in the face of executive intransigence. Thus it has been in the interests of the executive to compromise. As the legislative history to follow illustrates, the congressional will to oppose controversial executive arms proposals did not die with the legislative veto. Rather, Congress has turned to alternative means to voice its opposition. While legislators may not ultimately be willing to kill arms sales proposals, they are willing to pass resolutions of disapproval and direct counter-legislation, raising the profile of conflict and seriously damaging executive credibility with Arab nations in the Middle East.

## Conflict Between the Branches

The primary weapon which Congress had used to influence the process of policy making in arms sales to the Middle East had been the legislative veto. In the face of executive unwillingness to consult with Congress, much less compromise, on such important foreign policy decisions, the legislative veto provided Congress with unique leverage to compel cooperation (Grimmett, 1982).

As Franck and Weisband wrote of the Nelson-Bingham Amendment which provided for the legislative veto of arms sales, the

> initiative worked a profound transformation in arms export policy. [Though] no arms sale has actually been vetoed by Congress...the law has had a very significant impact on U.S. government policy, both on long-range planning and on several major individual sales. It has also affected the approach to foreign arms purchases (Franck and Weisband, 1979, 99).

Even such opponents of the legislative veto as Gilmour and Craig recognize that

> as exercised by Congress the [legislative veto] procedure has not been used to thwart arms sales proposed by the president; rather the threat of a veto has forced the president on several occasions to make proposals more acceptable by adjusting numbers, eliminating components, or attaching stipulations on use of the weapons. The result has been a consultation and negotiations process between the president and Congress (Gilmour and Craig, 1984, 375).

When the legislative veto was ruled unconstitutional the executive lost the incentive to cooperate with Congress in arms sales policy. Though some opposition was expected, in the end the administration assumed that it could count on a high probability of success for its proposals without having to compromise. In essence the president was willing to play a game of chicken with Congress.

Congress, for its part, took up the challenge. Unwilling to acquiesce to executive steamrolling, in the wake of the *Chadha* decision Congress has turned to joint resolutions of disapproval and counter-legislation to assert its role in arms sales policy. The number of bills and resolutions introduced in opposition to the presidents arms sales proposals reveals the congressional reaction. As Figure 5.1 illustrates, in the aftermath of the *Chadha* decision, the number of opposition bills and resolutions introduced on the issue of arms sales as a percentage of all bills and resolutions introduced in a given Congress jumps dramatically. Having lost the legislative veto as a tool of influence in such a conflictive area of foreign policy, Congress turned to this alternative means to retain influence in the policy making process.

In fact, the first instance of congressional opposition forcing the withdrawal of an executive arms sale proposal has come in the aftermath of *Chadha*. Where the threat of the legislative veto would previously have induced consultation and compromise on controversial arms sales, the showdown atmosphere which has developed between Congress and the executive since 1983 has led to dramatic displays of Congress' resolve. Administration officials argue that the result has been to undermine confidence in American unity on policy, embarrass recipient governments, and lend leverage to hostile states in the region. As one member of the State Department described the furious debate which resulted from President Bush's attempts to ram through a massive arms sale to Saudi Arabia in the wake of the Iraqi invasion of Kuwait:

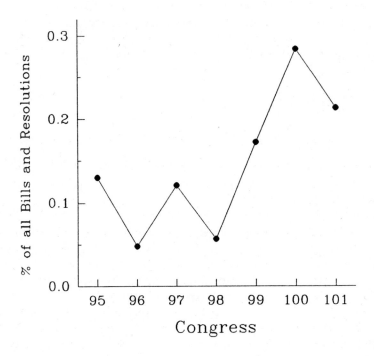

FIGURE 5.1   Bills and Resolutions: Arms Sales to the Middle East (95th-101st Congress).

the repercussions over conflict over the Saudi sale looks like Congress is not supportive of executive policy there. The Saudis react to that and the Iraqis are already making political hay out of it. In their world it is unacceptable for a leader to be rebuffed in that way...humiliating. It makes the U.S. look as if we are not united in foreign policy terms, looks like Israel has a veto over U.S.-Arab relations, has negative implications for the Saudi government, and foreign policy costs in general.

Though there has always been policy disagreement between Congress and the president over arms sales to the Middle East, the major consequence of *Chadha* has been to force that conflict out into the open. Instead of resolving disagreements through behind-the-scenes compromise, conflict has been brought into full public view as Congress takes dramatic action by passing resolutions of disapproval or legislation countering executive proposals. The profile of conflict has been raised.

A detailed look at trends in congressional-executive relations from the introduction of the legislative veto to the present will illustrate the importance of the tool for resolving conflict and the destructive impact of its loss.

## Arms Sales to the Arabs and U.S. Policy in the Middle East

In the twentieth century, commitment to the establishment and preservation of the Jewish state in the land formerly known as Palestine has been the overriding goal of U.S. policy toward the Middle East. Beginning in 1973, however, "U.S. policy reflected an awareness among policy makers and informed citizens that "the Arab case" deserved more sympathetic consideration and that a number of Arab grievances against Israel were well-founded" (Crabb and Holt, 1989, 98). Executive policy makers, particularly the State Department, sought to take a more evenhanded approach toward the Arab-Israeli conflict. Congress remained the focal point of support for Israel. The rift has made arms sales to Arab nations in the Middle East a flash point in the congressional-executive struggle over the determination of American foreign policy.

### Congress Gets Involved

In 1974 U.S. arms sales abroad hit an all-time high. Sales, cash and credit, totalled $10.8 billion in that year, more than ten times the total for 1970 (*CQ Almanac*, 1975, 356). The vast majority of these sales went to South Asia and the Middle East.

The virtual explosion of arms sales to Arab nations in the Middle East prompted accusations in Congress that American supplies of weapons to both Israel and its hostile neighbors was creating a run-away arms race in the region. Moreover, critics argued, sales of military equipment had become a critical instrument for executive reorientation of American foreign policy without consulting Congress. "The current military sales program is not the product of a careful and deliberate policy arrived at through joint action by Congress and the executive branch," complained Sen. Hubert Humphrey (D-Minn), "it has developed through its own momentum" (*CQ Almanac*, 1975, 357).

That year Congress passed the Nelson-Bingham Amendment to the Foreign Aid Authorization for fiscal year 1975. This amendment required the president to formally notify Congress of any proposed arms sale exceeding $25 million 20 days in advance. It further gave Congress the ability to block any proposed arms sale by legislative veto (concurrent resolution). In 1981 the Arms Export Control Act lowered the amount triggering the notification requirement from $25 million to $7 million, substantially increasing the number of sales subject to review and tightening Congress' grip.

The first confrontation between Congress and the president over arms sales came on July 10, 1975, with President Ford's notification of his intention to sell 14 batteries of Hawk ground-to-air missiles, 8 batteries of Vulcan anti-aircraft guns, and Redeye shoulder-fired missiles to Jordan. The sophistication of the Hawk missiles and their potential use as offensive weapons against Israel drew immediate fire from Congress.

The president's initial reluctance to compromise changed in the face of clear opposition from both the House and Senate foreign affairs committees. Resolutions to disapprove the sale were introduced in both Houses. Congress was serious about the Nelson-Bingham Amendment and a showdown seemed imminent.

After a summer of intense negotiations Congress and the president came to a compromise-- one which left deep scars on American-Jordanian relations. On September 16 Ford withdrew the original sale proposal and substituted a revised, compromise proposal. Through negotiations between Secretary of State Henry Kissinger, Under Secretary of State Joseph Sisco and Sens. Clifford Case (R-N.J.) and Jonathan Bingham (D-N.Y.) an understanding had been reached which provided assurances that the weapons would be used only for defensive purposes. Despite objections from Jordan's King Hussein, Ford sent a formal letter to Congress September 17 pledging that the missiles would be used only as "defensive and nonmobile antiaircraft weapons" (*CQ Almanac*, 1975, 359). In return Congress agreed to drop efforts to cut the number of missiles sold.

Humiliated by the public scrutiny of his nation's ability to handle the sophisticated weaponry, Jordan's King Hussein called off the arms deal shortly after the compromise was announced. Though the deal was later reinstated, it was clear that the open conflict between Congress and the president had caused serious damage both at home and abroad.

This first test of Congress' will to confront the president on arms sales, though embarrassing to all parties, did serve to teach valuable lessons for the future. The major problem, as Congress saw it, was that the Ford Administration had sought to present Congress with a *fait accompli*. While agreeing to the formal notification requirements, the administration had already taken the arms deal to its final stages, leaving Congress little room to participate. Determined to give force to the Nelson-Bingham Amendment, Congress forced the president into a choice between compromise or confrontation. The upshot set the tone for the new accommodations the president would have to make with Congress. It clearly demonstrated

> the weakness of a procedure that encourages an administration to commit itself to foreign sales in secret, then face Congress with a choice between acquiescence or the public humiliation of a friendly government. The Hawk crisis showed that the administration should seek congressional advice much earlier in the process: *before* a decision is reached on large-scale weapons sales to a foreign government (Franck and Weisband, 1979, 103).

The lesson appeared to sink in, as demonstrated the next year when the administration spent "weeks of preparatory consultation on Capitol Hill" before giving formal notification March 25 of its intention to sell six C-130 transport planes to Egypt (*CQ Almanac*, 1976, 237). Key legislators, Hubert Humphrey (D-Minn.) and Jacob Javits (R-N.Y.), agreed not to introduce resolutions of disapproval in exchange for assurances from Kissinger that no further military equipment would be sold to Egypt in 1976, and that the deal "is an individual step and does not set a precedent" for extensive arms sales to Egypt in the future (*CQ Almanac*, 1976, 237).

Similarly, when threats of legislative vetoes arose in response to the administration's September 1 proposal to sell 160 F-16 jet fighter planes to Iran and 1,500 Maverick missiles to Saudi Arabia, the administration entered into negotiations with Congress. Despite compromises reached between the administration and key Congressmen reducing the number of Mavericks to Saudi Arabia from 1,500 to 650, resolutions of disapproval were introduced in both houses and appeared to have had momentum.

It is difficult to know whether further compromise would have resolved the conflict. In what appeared to be a calculated manipulation of the debate, Secretary of State Henry Kissinger testified before the Senate Foreign Relations Committee that disapproval of the sale would lead to higher petroleum prices for American consumers. The implication was that Saudi Arabia had threatened American oil supplies. The committee immediately withdrew the resolution and the sale went through. Kissinger later admitted that Saudi Arabia had not, in fact, threatened to embargo oil shipments to the United States (*CQ Almanac*, 1976, 256).

Thus, while some progress was being made to effect cooperation between Congress and the executive, the path was not always smooth. Congress felt that existing requirements on the president were insufficient to guarantee a meaningful role for Congress in arms sales policy, while the administration remained strongly opposed to Congress' intrusive actions.

In order to increase congressional control of the process, in 1976 Congress for the first time separated authorization for economic and humanitarian aid from authorization for military aid and sales programs. By passing the two authorizations individually, the legislature could restrict executive actions specifically with regard to military aid without jeopardizing other elements of the U.S. foreign aid program. Congress then attached numerous provisions to the 1976 Foreign Military Assistance Act. They included: (1) giving Congress control over commercial as well as governmental arms sales; (2) imposing a ceiling on total annual arms sales of $9 billion dollars; (3) extending formal notification requirements for arms sales to 30 days from 20 days; (4) lowering the required amount from $25 billion to $7 billion; and (5) giving Congress the right to veto by concurrent resolution any arms proposal to nations which violated human rights.

Ford vetoed the bill, arguing that its passage would make Congress "a virtual co-administrator of foreign policy" (precisely what Congress had intended) (*CQ Almanac*, 1976, 213). He argued,

> I act as any President would and must retain the ability to function as the foreign policy leader and spokesman of the nation. In world affairs today, America can have only one foreign policy. Moreover, that foreign policy must be certain, clear and consistent (*CQ Almanac*, 1976, 225).

Congress subsequently passed a revised version which excluded the ceiling on total sales, control over commercial sales, and the ability to terminate sales to human rights abusers by concurrent resolution. The revised version (HR 13680) did retain the new $7 million notification requirement, the extended period for notification and a new provision which required all commercial sales above $7 million for major military equipment or $25 million for other military items to be reviewed and supervised by the government. In addition, the bill required much more frequent and detailed reporting by the administration concerning the justification for, and probable impact of, all present and anticipated arms sales. The bill also included a provision for the president to waive restrictions on the grounds of national security.

The next major test of Congress' participation in arms sales came with President Carter's July 7, 1977, proposal to sell seven Airborne Warning and Control System (AWACS) planes to Iran. Though Iran had been a fairly reliable ally under the Shah, the prospect of sending AWACS to the Middle East represented a qualitative shift in arms technology in the region. Three objections formed the basis of controversy in Congress over the sale: (1) that the AWACS would give Iran a significant military advantage in the region, an advantage which other Arab states might seek to employ against Israel; (2) the danger of AWACS technology, the most sophisticated in the American arsenal, falling into Soviet or terrorist hands; and (3) the need to deploy a large number of American military personnel in Iran to train the Iranians, and the danger that Americans might become involved in hostilities in the Middle East.

Ignoring requests from Senate Majority Leader Robert Byrd (D-W.Va.) to withdraw the proposal, the administration continued to pursue the sale. On July 22 the House International Relations Committee unexpectedly passed a resolution of disapproval, and danger loomed that the Senate Foreign Relations Committee might do the same. Carter withdrew the proposal on July 28, and negotiations began. One of the administration's greatest tasks was to allay congressional fears that Iranian arms acquisition was not out of control. Following President Nixon's unilateral decision in 1972 to sell Iran all the arms it desired, Iran had become the single largest purchaser of U.S. military equipment, acquiring $10.4 billion worth between 1972 and 1976 (Purvis and Baker, 1984, 125).

A compromise was reached when the administration agreed to withhold some of the most sophisticated communications and coding gear from the planes and announced the Iranian government's pledges to provide significantly increased security for the equipment. Despite some lingering opposition to the sale, the deal was approved and delivery of the AWACS was scheduled to begin in 1981. Congressional reservations in this instance proved prophetic, as the Shah was overthrown only two years later in 1979. Delivery of the AWACS was never made.

An appreciation for the necessity of cooperating with Congress, however objectionable it may be, was evident in the Carter Administration's approach the following year. In 1978 Carter compiled a $4.8 billion package of arms sales to Saudi Arabia, Israel, and Egypt. Before the proposal was ever even submitted to Congress, Carter agreed to hold off formal notification until after Congress had cleared away debate over the Panama Canal treaties. This conciliatory gesture allowed Congress the full 30 days to act on the proposal without the burden of other major legislation pending.

A second compromise was made soon thereafter when several members of Congress objected to the proposal as a package and called for each component to be considered separately. Specifically at issue was the sale of 60 F-15 interceptor jet fighters to Saudi Arabia, at the time among the world's most sophisticated aircraft. In what appeared to be a relatively gratuitous show of muscle flexing to capitalize on the president's evident attempts to be conciliatory, Senate Majority Leader Byrd intimated that each of the package's components stood a better chance of passage if the president would "drop the semantic buzz words 'all or nothing' package" (*CQ Almanac*, 1978, 408). Rep. Steven Solarz (D-N.Y.) likewise chimed in that his count "conclusively shows that there are votes to defeat the administration's proposed arms package in the absence of any effort on the part of the administration to reach a compromise" (*CQ Almanac*, 1978, 408). Carter backed off of earlier statements that the package must be considered as a whole and agreed to individual consideration of each sale.

In the end, the president won approval for his proposals with relatively minor changes. The most significant change was the inclusion of 20 extra F-15 jets for Israel, to be delivered between 1983-84, in order to even the balance between Saudi Arabia and Israel at 60 F-15s apiece. In addition the Pentagon and Saudi Arabia provided assurances that the Saudi F-15s would be used solely for defensive purposes.

What is noteworthy about all of these compromises is that they were often reached through assurances that a given recipient country would take particular security precautions, or that the weapons would be used only for defensive purposes. At times the actual number of weapons was cut, but more often the compromise hinged upon these intangibles. What made Congress willing to accept these assurances and approve the sales was the knowledge that if agreements or understandings were betrayed Congress could cut off funding or halt delivery of weapons (many of which were delivered over a period of years).

Probably more important, however, was the Congress' sense of itself as a participant in the process. The very fact that Congress never used its potential clout to completely block any arms sales is evidence that it did not really want to *take over* military sales policy from the president. Congress wanted an active part in the decision making process but did not want to shoulder the ultimate responsibility for American foreign policy.

Ronald Reagan's 1981 proposal to sell five AWACS aircraft to Saudi Arabia is illustrative of these points. Knowing that it faced a strong uphill battle to gain approval for AWACS sales to Saudi Arabia, the Reagan Administration skillfully crafted a way to satisfy Congress' desire for participation while preserving the original goals of the arms sale.

First, not only did the administration give Congress the formal notification period of 30 days, *and* the informal (but now standard) notification period of 20 days, they added another several days on top of that. This extra long notification period signaled to Congress the administration's intention to bring them in on the process. It also left the administration time to deflect any fatal opposition which might arise.

Second, the administration provided Congress with details of the sale which would normally have been classified. Again, the signal to Congress was that they were being taken seriously and were truly a party to the arms sale negotiations.

As expected, the proposal did meet with controversy on Capitol Hill, particularly in the House. The sale of AWACS to the Middle East had always inspired fear of escalating the regional arms race or that the technology would fall into the wrong hands. Though Saudi Arabia was a main supplier of American oil, many on Capitol Hill questioned the extent to which that country could be trusted to act in accordance with American interests. Staunch supporters of Israel, of course, continued their assertions that providing AWACS to Arab nations would seriously undermine the Jewish state's military position.

During the course of the debate the House did in fact pass a resolution disapproving the sale. This was expected, and the administration did relatively little to avert the vote (*CQ Almanac*, 1981, 136). Instead, the president concentrated his efforts on the Senate. Meetings were scheduled between administration officials and senators in which reservations about the sale were discussed. The administration began the draft of a letter addressing these reservations, but purposely "kept the text of the letter open until the day of the vote so it could be altered to meet the concerns of as many Senators as possible" (*CQ Almanac*, 1981, 138).

During the course of the debate, October 6, Egyptian President Anwar Sadat was assassinated by Arab extremists for his willingness to negotiate with Israel. Though tragic, the event boosted administration arguments for the need to shore up strong ties to moderate Arab nations in addition to Egypt.

On the day the Senate was scheduled to vote on the resolution of disapproval the president sent his letter to Congress. In it he assured legislators that Saudi Arabia had agreed to ensure the security of all

AWACS aircraft, share all information gathered from the technology with the U.S., *not* share the same information with any third country, and to operate the AWACS only over Saudi territory (meaning not in a manner threatening to Israel). Addressing many senators' desire for joint American-Saudi control over the AWACS on Saudi soil, the president assured that "agreements as they concern the organizational command and control structure for the operation of AWACS are of a nature to guarantee that the commitments above will be honored" (*CQ Almanac*, 1981, 136). In other words, he did not assure joint control, though taken together the assurances in the letter could be argued to satisfy joint control concerns.

The president's efforts were successful, and by a 48-52 vote the Senate rejected the resolution to disapprove (and effectively veto) the AWACS. Even former opponents of the sale noted the critical importance the president's letter had had in allowing senators to claim that they had wrested concessions from the administration without actually changing the contents of the sale (*CQ Almanac*, 1981, 137). Foreign Relations Committee Chairman Charles Percy (R-Ill.) said, "the letter was very important. It was an assurance Senators wanted" (*CQ Almanac*, 1981, 138). Majority Leader Howard Baker (R-Tenn) likewise commended the White House's cooperation and "extraordinary" consultation with Congress, addressing their concerns and providing the necessary assurances which allowed them to vote for the sale (*CQ Almanac*, 1981, 136).

Though cooperation was often grudging and the relationship sometimes rocky, Congress and the executive had come to an overall accommodation on arms sales. In general, the White House came to accept the need to include Congress in the process of arms sales *before* the deal was signed and sealed. Congress would have to flex its legislative veto muscle from time to time, but was generally satisfied with assurances that Israel's interests would be protected and that the arms race in the Middle East was under control. On the surface these may not appear to be very substantive gains on the part of Congress. The president still initiated the vast majority of agreements and despite some strong debate was never stymied by the Congress.

What was critical to the relationship was the sense of participation gained by Congress and the *ability* (even if unused) to block final action. Though concern for the protection of Israel was a constant in congressional consideration of arms sales proposals, in general the *substance* of compromises was less important than the fact that compromise had been achieved. The leverage gained through the legislative veto was the critical element compelling presidential compromise and instilling a sense of congressional efficacy. It was the base upon which congressional-executive cooperation lay.

## From Cooperation to Conflict:
## The Irony of Reform

The 1983 *Chadha* decision not only nullified the legislative veto but seriously undermined the basis for cooperation between the president and Congress over arms sales to the Middle East. The year after the Supreme Court ruling Congress for the first time dealt a fatal blow to an executive arms sale proposal. The outcome was symptomatic of the conflict that lay ahead as Congress and the president once again fought for influence over foreign policy.

In order to maintain its codeterminative gains, Congress turned to other measures which would serve as substitutes for the legislative veto. One of the first tests of these substitutes came when Reagan announced February 29, 1984, his intention to sell 1,200 Stinger missiles and 400 launchers to Saudi Arabia, and 1,613 Stinger missiles and 315 launchers to Jordan. At a cost of $141 million and $133 million respectively, both arms sales required the notification to Congress 30 days prior to the sale. Yet the *Chadha* decision had taken away Congress' ability to block the sale through concurrent resolution.

The sale of Stingers to Jordan was particularly contentious given recent skirmishes in the press with King Hussein who had called U.S. policies a stumbling block to peace in the Middle East. To maintain its leverage in opposing the sale to Jordan the House Foreign Affairs committee adopted an amendment to the 1984-85 foreign aid authorization bill (HR 5119) banning any sales of advanced arms to Jordan until that country agreed to negotiate with and recognize Israel (*CQ Almanac*, 1984, 116; and see "Foreign Aid Bill," 104). Overwhelming support for the amendment left little doubt about the prospects for successful override should the president decide to veto the bill.

For the first time a president had been thwarted by Congress in an arms sale. Reagan withdrew the proposal. Instead of the haggling which had become a standard part of congressional-executive negotiations, both parties had staked their positions. The president made no compromises, Congress made no concessions, and Jordan lost the missiles.

Later that month, as the war in the Persian Gulf escalated, the president invoked the national security clause to send 400 missiles to the Saudis. Under the "emergency" provision of the International Securities Assistance Act of 1979 (PL 96-92) he waived the required prior notification of Congress. Two days later, May 30, Reagan sent formal notification of the sale to Congress along with the required justification for the emergency powers. Immediate and vocal protests arose from Congress charging Reagan with abuse of emergency powers. Senate Appropriations Subcommittee on Foreign Operations Chairman Robert Kasten (R-Wisc.) accused the administration of "at very least abus(ing) the consulting process...making bizarre decisions and of misusing the president's emergency powers to sidestep Congress in making foreign arms sales" (*CQ Almanac*, 1984, 118).

Attempts to regain the cooperative spirit between the branches failed miserably the next year, resulting in yet another defeat for the president over a proposed sale of arms to Jordan. On September 27, 1985, Reagan sent informal notification to Congress of his intention to sell between $1.5 billion and $2 billion worth of arms. It would have been the largest sale ever to Jordan and one of the largest ever to an Arab country (*CQ Almanac*, 1985, 94). The conflict began immediately after the announcement when Sens. Kasten (R-Wisc.) and Inouye (D-Hawaii) protested that Secretary of State George Shultz had lied to them. In exchange for their support of a recently passed economic aid package to Jordan, free of restriction on arms sales, the senators maintained that Shultz had promised to consult with Congress prior to any arms agreements with that country. The proposal submitted had clearly been worked out in detail and harkened back to the days of White House proposals submitted to Congress as practically *faits accomplis*. In a letter to Shultz, Kasten wrote that the failure to consult signaled "a significant deterioration of relations between you and your department and the Appropriations Committee" (*CQ Almanac*, 1985, 94).

The failure to consult with Congress may in fact have been a calculated decision given at least two components of the sale: 12 *mobile* Hawk anti-aircraft missile batteries; and conversion of Jordan's 14 currently immobile Hawk batteries into mobile units. Inclusion of these two items constituted a direct repudiation of the spirit of the compromise reached between Congress and the executive in 1974 when Congress agreed to the sale of immobile Hawk missiles to Jordan. In their mobile form, Hawk missiles could easily be brought within range of Israel, transforming their capabilities from defensive to offensive.

The administration strategy backfired October 21, shortly after the proposal was formally introduced, when the Senate voted 97-1 to reject the sale. In a compromise gesture (S J Res 228), however, they agreed to allow the sale only after March 1, 1986, "unless direct and meaningful peace negotiations between Israel and Jordan are under way" (*CQ Almanac*, 1985, 95). Shortly after the Senate vote the House agreed to the

Senate resolution, though they could likely have passed a much tougher bill. As *Congressional Quarterly Almanac* reported,

> the Foreign Affairs panel had approved the measure by voice vote, even though a majority of its members, and more than 280 House members, had supported a much tougher House measure (H J Res 428) that would have blocked the sale indefinitely. But the panel settled for the Senate resolution, with no changes, because it was the only legislation with a chance of being enacted into law by Nov. 20, when a 30-day period for congressional review of the sale was to expire. If Congress had not acted by then, Reagan would have been free to carry out the sale. Administration officials warned that Reagan might go ahead with the sale, if he had the choice, to assert his executive authority (1985, 95).

The report added,

> The Senate's action was the sharpest rebuke the Republican-led chamber had administered to Reagan on a major foreign policy issue since June 1984, when it denied funds for anti-government "contras" in Nicaragua (1985, 95).

Faced with overwhelming opposition and the threat of losing the sale altogether if he vetoed the resolution, Reagan reluctantly signed the bill delaying the sale. Though a compromise had been worked out, the president came out of the battle badly bruised. His wounds were compounded further that year when, in separate deals, Congress forced the president to delete completely Stinger missiles, F-15 fighter aircraft and M-1 tanks from a Saudi arms package (Crabb and Holt, 1989, 118). It was clear that Congress had no intention of returning to the days when the White House could present a completed arms deal to Congress and count on its approval for the sake of saving face internationally. At the same time, the president was trying to take full advantage of the loss of the legislative veto to minimize the need to consult with Congress.

On April 18, 1986, Reagan formally notified Congress of another plan to sell Saudi Arabia an arms package totalling $265 million. Though Reagan agreed not to include the contentious Stinger missiles in the deal, tensions still ran high over Congress' ability to control escalating arms sales to the Arabs.

The depth of hostility between the branches was dramatized by the overwhelming passage of a joint resolution of disapproval in both Houses on May 6th and 7th. As expected, the president vetoed the resolution and the battle was on.

As a substitute to the legislative veto the joint resolution of disapproval is probably the hardest to sustain. It requires a two-thirds vote in both houses *and* is subject to presidential veto. By contrast, the concurrent resolution provided for in the legislative veto was not subject to presidential veto. Were the mechanism still constitutional the vote on the Saudi arms package would have constituted the first *floor* defeat of a presidential initiative in arms sales (as opposed to defeat imposed by forcing the president to withdraw the proposal).

But would the Congress have actually used the legislative veto to kill the arms sale if it were still constitutional? Probably not. Though clairvoyance in such matters is rare, a strong argument can be made that this was a case of congressional-executive brinkmanship catalyzed by Congress' desire to make itself heard.

With the well-founded expectation that Reagan would veto the joint resolution of disapproval, members were free to make a strong point by voting against the president. They knew that another vote would come along before the sale was killed. In order for Congress to ultimately block the arms deal both houses would have to override his veto by a two-thirds majority. In the shadow of an upcoming election, a vote of disapproval also proved politically expedient for members of both parties wary about the wrath of AIPAC, the very powerful pro-Israel lobby.

When it came to overriding the veto, however, Reagan ultimately triumphed. Though he only averted an override by one vote in the Senate (66-34), Senate Foreign Relations Committee Chairman Lugar admitted that he had several backup votes to save the president if necessary (*CQ Almanac*, 1986, 377; *CQ Weekly Report*, June 7, 1986, 1262). While many members wanted to ensure consultation and congressional participation in the arms sale they did not necessarily want to undermine the president completely.

As James Exon (D-Neb.) argued, "The security interests of the United States rest with sustaining the veto. Today we have the leader of the free world laying his prestige on the line. That makes it a considerably different situation" (*CQ Almanac*, 1986, 377).

The significance of the Saudi arms deal is not the ultimate success or failure of the president. Rather, it illustrates the rigidity imposed upon the debate when Congress is compelled to use alternative means to the legislative veto to assert itself. While the compromise under the legislative veto was often contentious, it had become regularized. Each party understood the grandstanding and horse-trading involved and had a fair idea of what to expect from the other. It was an N-round game in which repeated meetings led to a long term equilibrium. Without the legislative veto the game changes each time. The alternative means of control chosen by Congress determines the degree of flexibility which each side is willing, and able, to concede. Yet as each issue arises there is no constant incentive for concessions. A joint resolution of disapproval precipitates a public game of chicken while the implementation of countering legislation effectively nips either side's flexibility in the bud. Informal provisions allow for the greatest degree of flexibility but are dependent upon the conciliatory spirit of the president--a spirit less and less likely as relations continue to erode. Secretary of State Shultz' broken pledge in the Jordanian arms sale is a case in point. Each side is left to guard itself and the probability of conflict is increased.

Contrasting President Ford's attempts to sell Maverick anti-tank missiles to Saudi Arabia in 1976 with a similar attempt by Reagan in 1987 further illustrates the rigidity which alternatives to the legislative veto impose upon the congressional-executive debate over arms sales. In the earlier episode an agreement was reached to reduce the number of Mavericks sold. Congress' requirements for consultation and compromise were satisfied and the president's proposal was passed. In 1987 the relationship between Congress and the president was different. Charges that Reagan was increasingly skirting Congress, undermining the spirit of codetermination, heightened defenses on both sides.

In a break with a decade-long tradition, the president ignored the 20 day informal notification period. This left Congress only the formal notification period of 30 days to act on the proposed sale. Opposition to the sale arose immediately. On June 10, even as Assistant Secretary of State Richard Murphy testified before the Senate Foreign Relations Committee on behalf of the sale, opponents were at work. Sens. Packwood (R-Oregon) and Cranston (D-Calif.) gathered 67 signatures on a proposal for a Senate resolution to disapprove the sale. The number was sufficient both to disapprove the sale and to override a presidential veto. Opponents in the House were likewise ready with a companion disapproval resolution containing over 200 signatures (*CQ Almanac*, 1987, 170). Still bruised from narrowly averting an override on the 1986 Saudi arms package, and uncertain about the prospects for repeating the trick in the now Democratically controlled Senate, the administration withdrew the Mavericks proposal.

Lingering hostility between the branches resurfaced the next year on June 8, 1988, when Reagan gave Congress informal notification of a proposed arms sale to Kuwait which included Maverick missiles. Voicing immediate opposition to the proposal, opponents led by Rep. Lawrence Smith (D-Fla.) asked the administration not to formally propose the sale at the end of the 20 days without significant progress in the Arab-Israeli peace negotiations. Ignoring the request, Reagan formally notified Congress July 7 of his intention to proceed with the sale. "By notifying Congress just a few days after the informal notice period expired, the administration appeared to signal unwillingness to negotiate with Congress (*CQ Almanac*, 1988, 507).

The president's determination was met in kind by Congress. The Senate adopted, without debate, an amendment to the foreign aid bill (HR 4637) blocking the sale of any Mavericks to Kuwait. In the House Smith and 103 co-sponsors introduced a resolution (H J Res 609) to block the entire sale. The air of conflict was heightened by the fact that the resolution was introduced July 12 as President Reagan was meeting with Kuwaiti Prime Minister Sheik Saad al-Sabah, pledging his best efforts to win congressional approval for the sale (*CQ Almanac*, 1988, 507).

The stage was set for another showdown. In this instance, however, a direct confrontation was derailed when the Kuwaitis announced the signing of an agreement to buy weapons from the Soviet Union. A week earlier Saudi Arabia had announced the purchase of approximately $25 billion worth of warplanes from Britain to replace those blocked by Congress the year earlier. And soon after that announcement it was revealed that the Saudis had secretly acquired Chinese intermediate range nuclear missiles capable of striking targets in Israel and throughout the Middle East.

The message was clear. Increasing conflict between Congress and the president threatened the U.S. position in the Middle East. In a show of cooperation reminiscent of pre-*Chadha* days the administration and House opponents forged a compromise and allowed the sale to go through. One hundred Maverick-D air-to-surface missiles (used mainly against tanks) were dropped from the proposal and replaced by an additional 100 Maverick-G anti-ship missiles (*CQ Almanac*, 1988, 507). Overcoming continued opposition from Arizona Senator Dennis DeConcini the Senate grudgingly agreed to the compromise.

The spirit of compromise forced upon Congress and the executive by the external threat of alternative arms suppliers was short-lived. The sophistication of the technology under consideration was such that U.S. arms could only occasionally be replaced by other countries. Moreover the easing of Cold War tensions had significantly reduced the fear of Soviet penetration in the Middle East.

AIPAC pressures continued to inspire disagreement over executive proposals to sell advanced weaponry to the Arabs. Despite attempts by some members of Congress to reduce restrictions on the president in some areas, the Subcommittee on Europe and the Middle East announced May 3, 1989, its vote to retain existing restrictions on arms sales to the Middle East (*CQ Weekly Report*, May 6, 1989, 1057). Moreover, both sides geared up for what promised to be the first big showdown of the Bush

Administration: a proposal to sell several dozen advanced fighter jets to Saudi Arabia (*CQ Weekly Report*, November 11, 1989, 3096).

The next year the conflict was repeated as Bush Administration officials tried to slip through a massive arms package to Saudi Arabia totalling $21 billion (touted as the largest single arms transfer in history) by riding the wave of pro-Saudi sentiment following the Iraqi invasion of Kuwait. Swift and vocal congressional opposition forced Bush to withdraw the proposal and postpone consideration of the sale (*Washington Post*, September 20, 1990, A1). The result was to undermine administration credibility among the Saudis and give the Iraqis embarrassing propaganda material.

Given the strategic importance of the issues under consideration and the salience of arms sales policy to powerful constituent groups, there is little reason to expect that the battles between Congress and the president are over. What is needed is a means to reconcile the inevitable conflict in as discreet a manner as possible. While the legislative veto could not eliminate conflict over arms sales to the Middle East, it was effective in compelling compromise and keeping conflict to a controlled level. In its absence, the increased profile of conflict has damaged both the process and the credibility of American foreign policy.

# 6

## Comity or Latent Conflict?: Most Favored Nation Trade Status

As an intermestic issue, most-favored-nation (MFN) trade status combines both foreign and domestic policy. Trade is a powerful tool of American foreign policy. But by its very nature, it is also of critical importance to American business. The ramifications of U.S. trade relations are integral to the workings of the American economy, and consequently are of fundamental importance in domestic policy.

The president and Congress often face similar public pressures on intermestic issues. This is particularly the case in issues of foreign economic policy, such as trade, foreign aid and investment (Pastor, 1980) where both have "reasonably well-established corporate views" (Ripley and Franklin, 1984, 228). As a consequence, often times congressional and executive policy views will coincide. Other times, however, they will conflict. Indeed, as the case of MFN trade status illustrates, it is even possible for policy views to remain generally coincident until some external variable affects the pressures faced by either legislators or the president (or both), driving a wedge between policy stances. The combination of domestic and foreign policy concerns inherent in intermestic issues strongly motivates Congress to have a hand in policy making, particularly when there is disagreement over what form American policy should take. Consequently, the potential for conflict between the branches is high. A statutory tool which can facilitate resolution of policy conflict is essential to an effective policy process. As the case of MFN trade status demonstrates, here too the loss of the legislative veto has had an unintended and detrimental impact on interbranch conflict and the formulation of American foreign policy.

### Formulating Most-Favored-Nation Trade Policy

The case of MFN trade status illustrates another instance in which the *Chadha* decision has resulted in a heightened profile of conflict between the legislative and executive branches. This case presents an added dimension, however, in that the increased conflict following the loss of the legislative veto came in two stages: one motivated primarily by institutional concerns, the next compounded by the mobilization of public opinion. Immediately following the *Chadha* decision, legislators recognized the threat which the ruling posed to Congress' ability to retain influence over MFN policy. An increase in the number of bills and resolutions introduced to oppose or restrict the president's ability to extend MFN is the manifestation of these concerns. Still, these concerns were motivated by institutional concerns rather than by reelection concerns. As such, though members of Congress were willing to oppose executive proposals, they lacked the incentive to take these policy disputes far enough to seriously threatening to nullify an executive initiative. In 1989 the context surrounding the debate over MFN policy changed, adding a strong reelection motive for congressional assertion in this issue area. Specifically, public outrage over the massacre in China's Tienanmen Square and the Soviet crackdowns in the Baltic States provided the electoral motivation to legislators to credibly threaten the president's proposed extensions of trade benefits to these counties. While the institutional motivation had always been present, the lack of strong electoral motivation had kept members (and thus Congress as a whole) from becoming assertive in this area of foreign policy. With public opinion now serving as a catalyst, the preconditions for a heightened degree of congressional-executive conflict have been satisfied. Congressional assertion, coupled with the will to actively oppose the president's policy proposals have led Congress to search the statutory mechanisms available to it to press its policy position. Lacking the legislative veto, members have been driven to introduce numerous resolutions of disapproval and direct counter-legislation in the effort to compel serious executive consideration of their objections. Numerous hearings have been held, particularly concerning MFN status for China, and the entire profile of conflict over the issue has been further elevated.

The lesson to be learned from this case is that the degree of conflict which results from the loss of the legislative veto is contingent upon the factors motivating each branch, and that these factors themselves may change over time. In some cases, as we shall see in the example of war powers, the nature of the issue is such that the likelihood of these conditions ever being met is minimal. In such cases one can argue with considerable confidence that *Chadha* has not, and will not, have much impact on interbranch relations. On issues such as MFN, however, the "intermestic" nature of the issue carries with it the potential that exogenous factors (in this case Chinese and Soviet governmental actions, and the ensuing groundswell of American public opinion) will affect the motivations of legislators, and lead Congress to assert itself in an area of interbranch disagreement. It is the means by which the two branches are able to resolve that conflict which determines the impact of the *Chadha* decision. Once again, we see that blanket statements dismissing the importance of the *Chadha* decision may be premature and misleading.

## Determining the Potential for Conflict

A closer look at the specific factors which affect interbranch relations in MFN trade policy will help to clarify the variable impact of *Chadha* and why its effects are now an important aspect of American foreign trade policy.

### Institutional Motives for Congressional Action

Article I, Section 8 of the Constitution gives Congress the power to "regulate commerce with foreign nations." Participation in the determination of trade agreements between the United States and foreign nations, is, therefore, clearly in the institutional interests of Congress. MFN trade status, ironically named, provides for reciprocal agreement between the U.S. and a trading partner that that partner should receive no less favorable trade treatment than any other U.S. trade partner. In other words, the trade relationship is not unique by its preferential treatment. The irony of the term "most-favored" is that those trading partners who do *not* have this status are unique in the negative terms of their trade relationship. Those without MFN status face substantially higher tariff barriers to their exports to the United States than do MFN nations. Delegation of MFN status, or more critically, denial of this status can prove a powerful tool in the economic dimension of American foreign policy.

MFN status had been generally granted to American trading partners since 1934. In 1951, the aftermath of WWII and the dawn of the Cold War, Congress passed legislation requiring the president to suspend MFN status to all countries in the Sino-Soviet bloc (Pregelj, 1990a; Harrison et al., 1990). In the effort to encourage independence from the Soviet Union,

Yugoslavia was exempted from the original suspension, as was Poland in 1960 under presidential discretionary authority. Keeping a firm rein on the determination of trade status, however, Congress in 1962 passed the Trade Expansion Act which eliminated such executive discretionary authority and made restoration of MFN status possible only by specific legislation (Crabb and Holt, 1989, 197).

As will be discussed in the chronology of MFN legislation below, Congress was willing to delegate a significant degree of power to the president to negotiate trade agreements in the 1960s and 1970s, including eventually the power to grant (waive the ban on) MFN status. It did, however, retain for itself the power to disapprove new grants of MFN status and renewal of MFN status (on an annual basis) via legislative veto. This amendment, initiated by Senator Henry Jackson (D-Wash.) and later Representative Charles Vanik (D-Ohio), would prove to be a major source of controversy in the early 1970s between Congress and the Nixon Administration.[7] While interbranch conflict over the question of MFN status had remained relatively minor in the years since the passage of Jackson-Vanik, recent events have brought the issue to the fore, once again raising questions of institutional power balance.

### Electoral Motives for Congressional Action

With an eye toward reelection, members of Congress were strongly motivated to act in support of the Jackson-Vanik amendment to the Trade Act of 1974 due in large part to the influence of the Jewish lobby in their constituencies who were eager to see the United States influence Soviet discrimination against the emigration of Soviet Jews. Although a close look at the inception of the amendment shows Senator Jackson to be the primary catalyst, his efforts to persuade other members to his position were strongly aided by the organized Jewish community, labor, and a variety of other interest groups (Stern, 1979). In fact it has been shown that the support of perhaps the strongest man in the Congress (if not all of Washington), Wilbur Mills, Chairman of the House Ways and Means Committee, was won through pressure from some of his prominent Jewish constituents (Stern, 1979; Caldwell, 1981).

In the years between the passage of Jackson-Vanik and 1989, however, there was little electoral motivation for members to become greatly involved in MFN policy making. Of the countries which were under consideration for MFN waivers, primarily Hungary, Romania and China, only Romania was a constant source of dispute between Congress and the president. Though representatives' opposition to Romania's human rights record created a constant source of discontent, the administration maintained that strong economic ties to Romania was the best way to influence that nation and enhance its independence from the Soviet Union. Lacking a sufficient domestic constituency legislators were not strongly compelled to take on the president over Romania.

In 1989, however, the considerations changed.   Specifically, the Chinese government's June 3-4 attack of student pro-democracy demonstrators in Tienanmen Square raised the indignation and revulsion of the American people. Ironically, the week before the crackdown China's MFN waiver had been renewed for another year.  At the same time, political reform in the Soviet Union and the demise of the Cold War era led President Bush to announce his decision to extend MFN status to that country as well. But Soviet military  crackdowns on nationalistic movements in the Baltic Republics raised opposition both in Congress and the American public. The consensus of public opinion in their constituencies provided representatives with the electoral motivation to oppose the administration's proposed MFN waivers for China and the Soviet Union.

## Congressional Will to Act

Congressional action can result in varying degrees of conflict.  In the 1989 cases of China and the Soviet Union, unlike in previous policy disagreements over MFN, congressional motivation to influence policy was not easily dismissed. These two cases represented the first since the *Chadha* decision in which Congress had the will to strongly defy the president, though not the statutory leverage to do so.  Though there had been interbranch conflict resulting from the loss of the legislative veto, until this time there had not been a case sufficiently controversial to inspire legislation to convert the one-house and concurrent resolution of disapproval mechanisms to joint resolutions. The cases of China and the Soviet Union provided the inspiration.

The recognition of the impact which *Chadha* had on the legislature's leverage over MFN policy prompted passage of the Customs and Trade Act of 1990 which substitutes a joint resolution of disapproval for the presumably unconstitutional one-house and concurrent resolutions contained in the Trade Act of 1974.  As in the case of arms sales to the Middle East, the recognition of eroded congressional statutory power in MFN policy, coupled with substantial policy disagreement with the executive over China and the Soviet Union has prompted Congress to take measures to reassert itself.  These alternative measures, it will be argued, have further raised the profile of conflict between the branches.

*Conflict Between the Branches*

As in the other cases presented in this work, interbranch conflict over the issue of MFN trade status manifests itself in the form of an increase in the introduction of bills and resolutions intended to counter the president's proposal. There was a considerable amount of open conflict between Senator Jackson and the Nixon Administration in the period leading up to the passage of the Jackson-Vanik amendment, though most of this took place in the years preceding the scope of this study (1972 and 1973, the 93d Congress). From the 95th Congress to the 98th there was relatively little conflict as measured by opposition bills and resolutions. As Figure 6.1 demonstrates, however, in the period following the *Chadha* decision, the 99th and 100th Congresses, the number of conflictive bills

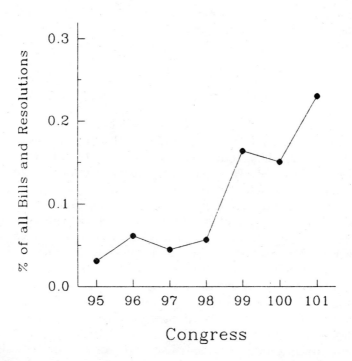

FIGURE 6.1 Bills and Resolutions: Most-Favored-Nation Trade Status (95th-101st Congress).

and resolutions took a precipitous rise. The number rose dramatically again in 1989 with the addition of an electoral motive to act, catalyzed by public outrage over Tienanmen Square and the situation in Lithuania.

International events, coupled with intense public opinion at home, inspired congressional assertion and congressional will to counter President Bush' intended policies of MFN renewal to China and MFN extension to the Soviet Union. The question now was how to do that effectively. It was at this point that the real import of the *Chadha* decision took on meaning in the realm of MFN policy.

Legislators now surveyed the statutory tools available to them in the effort to effectively influence MFN policy. Without the legislative veto Congress found itself at a structural disadvantage to compel executive consultation and compromise on policy matters. In essence, without congressional access to the legislative veto the executive had no incentive to compromise its position.

The most visible indication of congressional attempts to fortify its position vis-a-vis the executive was the passage of the Customs and Trade Act of 1990, substituting the joint resolution of disapproval for the now unconstitutional one-house and concurrent resolutions in the Trade Act of 1974. If it could not rely on the threat of the legislative veto to compel executive incorporation of congressional concerns into its MFN trade policy, Congress would be forced exercise the alternatives available to it--alternatives which, by their very nature, present public, high profile opposition to presidential policy.

The reelection motive also inspired congressional assertion in another form: committee and subcommittee hearings. These further served to raise the profile of interbranch conflict. As Figure 6.2 illustrates, the number of committee and subcommittee hearings held concerning MFN trade status soared in 1989. Though the strategy of holding hearings is not appropriate for all issue areas, in the case of MFN it provided legislators a dual means to demonstrate to the public a committment to human rights in China and a means to put added pressure on the president to heed its policy concerns.

It is difficult to assess what the level of conflict would have been had the legislative veto been available to Congress. Clearly, the executive branch would have had considerably more incentive to at least consult with, perhaps even compromise with, legislators. In the cases of China and the Soviet Union, public opinion formed such a strong foundation for congressional opposition that the legislative veto threat would have been very serious indeed.

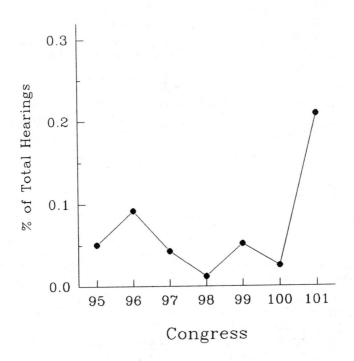

FIGURE 6.2 Hearings: Most-Favored-Nation Trade Status (95th-101st Congress).

The July 1991 House and Senate votes to limit China's MFN extension to one year demonstrate precisely the type of overt interbranch conflict which the legislative veto would serve to ameliorate. Were the legislative veto still operative these votes *could* have killed the president's proposal for a multi-year extension. The question is, *would* Congress have exercised the veto? Given the degree of public sympathy for its position, in the face of an unrelenting administration the legislature would very likely have passed the veto. But would the administration have remained unrelenting? Probably not. Given the strong likelihood of a veto, logic would compel the president to heed the representatives' concerns and incorporate at least some of the conditions into its proposal to extend MFN for China. These compromises would likely have been worked out before the president's final proposal was submitted and behind closed doors so as to conceal as much as possible the appearance of executive conciliation to the legislature. Though conflict would have existed, its profile would have been considerably lowered. (Whether Congress' ability to compel policy compromise is a positive or negative attribute of the legislative veto will be discussed in the concluding chapter. For the moment the point is merely that this potential power existed.)

The way the game is set up post-*Chadha*, however, the president can almost always count on the Senate, if not to vote with him on the original legislation then to sustain his veto. Thus, the executive has the incentive to go for broke. There may be a few bruises along the way in the form of tough rhetoric and even the initial passage of restrictive legislation, but in the end he will probably emerge triumphant. In this case there is every reason to expect that China's MFN status will be extended without serious restrictions despite clear congressional opposition.

Congress likewise has the incentive to go for broke. The only way that it will be able to make any impact on policy in the absence of the legislative veto is through counter-legislation. Numerous bills and resolutions are therefore introduced to place heavy restrictions on China's MFN status. Holding hearings can raise the profile of the issue, put pressure on the administration and, it is hoped, build support for the congressional opponents' point of view. Rhetoric is sharpened and conflict is intensified and brought into public view.

A detailed look at the history of MFN policy from 1974 to 1991 will help to illustrate how all of these factors fit together to form the current state of conflict between Congress and the president.

## Most Favored Nation Trade Status
## and U.S. Foreign Policy

In the resurgent climate of the 1970s trade policy became an obvious candidate for congressional limits on the president. Regulation of trade and commerce is clearly delegated to the Congress in the Constitution, and thus presented a clear opportunity to reiterate its institutional standing in foreign policy. Moreover, one representative, Senator Henry (Scoop) Jackson, saw in the issue of trade a ticket to electoral support (particularly the Jewish and labor votes) as well as a means to establish for himself a policy domain within Congress. He was able to gain national attention with the issue of Soviet emigration policy, rallying Jewish and labor groups in each state and district to press their own representatives to support his amendment to trade legislation. Thus, in 1974, with both institutional and electoral motivation on their side, majorities in both houses voted to limit executive discretion in MFN trade policy.

Section 402 of the Trade Act of 1974 allows the president to waive the prohibition against MFN status for any country if he determines that doing so would promote freedom of emigration in that country. Thus, this legislation loosens the provisions enacted in the 1962 Trade Expansion Act which had kept MFN status decisions firmly within the legislature. But representatives were not willing to allow this new executive discretion to go unchecked. The Jackson-Vanik amendment to the Trade Act of 1974 made both the granting of MFN status to non-market economies (NMEs) and annual extensions of MFN status contingent upon semi-annual executive reports to Congress certifying unrestrictive emigration policy. In addition, the Jackson-Vanik amendment allowed Congress to nullify executive grants or extensions of MFN status through legislative veto. Though there had been a number of incarnations of the amendment in its two and one half year struggle for enactment, the final version allowed the initial granting of MFN status to be vetoed by either house of Congress, and the extension of a waiver (lifting denial of MFN status) to be vetoed by concurrent resolution (PL 93-618).

The Jackson-Vanik amendment is often considered a classic example of the power of the Jewish lobby in the United States. A close look at the timing of the initial introduction and main actors moving the legislation along, however, reveals that while the freedom of Soviet Jewry was certainly a concern it was not the primary motivating force. Originally, Jackson's amendment to the trade agreement between the United States and the Soviet Union was as much an effort against detente and improved trade relations as it was a display of concern for Soviet Jews. In fact, the earliest draft of the amendment was written prior to the Soviet announcement of an education tax on emigres (a thinly disguised effort to prevent Jews from emigrating by making the costs exorbitant[8]) (Stern, 1979).

The amendment itself, and certainly the political machinations which resulted in its final enactment, illustrate the power of an individual congressman to gain support from his colleagues and *lead* relevant constituencies on an issue with significant potential for political payoff. By several accounts, Jackson's drive for this amendment was spurred by his quest for the Democratic presidential nomination and his recognition of the issue's potential to rally the support of a broad range of constituencies, including Jews, labor, intellectuals, anti-communists and human rights supporters (Stern, 1979; Caldwell, 1981). Though he did not, in the end, get the nomination, Jackson's calculations about diverse support were right on target. As Stern argues, the Jackson amendment

> attracted support from interests spanning America's political spectrum....the Jews found a champion for Soviet Jewish emigration. (George) Meany [then president of AFL-CIO] found a possible means to block passage of the Trade Reform Act as well as to express sympathy for Soviet Jewry and to retard the policy of detente with the Soviet Union, which featured among other things liberalization of Soviet-American trade (Stern, 1979, 196-210).

In addition, American liberal intellectuals in solidarity with their Soviet counterparts (who would have been most affected by the education tax) supported the amendment, as did conservative anti-communists against any sort of rapprochement with the Soviet Union. Then-National Security Advisor Henry Kissinger mused, "most ironically, the right's traditional anti-communism found an ally in the left's antipathy to Nixon and growing concern with human rights" (Kissinger, 1979, 1237).

As one legislator surmised, "there is no political advantage in not signing" the amendment (*New York Times*, April 6, 1973, 14). By rallying a broad range of interest groups within each state and district, Jackson and Vanik were able to create enough constituency-based pressure on their colleagues to inspire majority support in both houses for emigration requirements on MFN trade status. Representatives were electorally motivated to comply with constituency pressures and institutionally motivated to maintain a firm grip on trade policy. Passage of the Jackson-Vanik amendment was assured. Jackson and Vanik were able to gain 235 House cosponsors for the amendment which, by virtue of its status as revenue legislation, had to originate in the House. The amendment was reported out of the Ways and Means Committee October 10, 1973, and was passed by a vote of 319-80 in the House December 11, 1973. The entire Trade Bill, entitled the Trade Reform Act was passed with the Jackson-Vanik amendment included December 20, 1974, by both the House (323-36) and Senate (72-4) and sent to newly elected President Ford for signature.

The Nixon Administration had strongly opposed the amendment from its inception. In the overall foreign policy plan designed by Nixon and Kissinger, trade was to be used to stem the increasing Soviet expansionism which appeared to be gaining momentum in the 1970s. Rewards in trade were to come as a result of political concessions. By granting the Soviet Union MFN status in the trade agreement, Nixon and

Kissinger planned to gain the economic leverage to impose meaningful sanctions should the U.S.S.R. pursue a belligerent course in international affairs (Kissinger, 1979). Making MFN status dependent upon Soviet emigration policy, a domestic affair, they argued, would undermine greater foreign policy goals of containing Soviet international expansionism.

Granting MFN status (in return for repayment of the Soviet Union's lend-lease debt) as part of the more comprehensive trade agreement was, arguably, a strategic mistake on the part of the administration (Stern, 1979, 61). It gave Jackson inordinate power over a major piece of legislation which the administration wanted very much to pass and allowed him to maneuver the issue to his political advantage.

> (T)he administration tried at first to ignore Jackson and his amendment. Later, the administration tried getting around Jackson with concessions of the education tax. Still later, it had tried to confront the amendment head-on in the House of Representatives. All failed. Having lost the legislative battle, the administration had little alternative but to negotiate....Trilateral talks (among the administration, the Soviets and Jackson) began in Spring 1974 involving two branches of the U.S. government and a foreign power (Stern, 1979, 105).

While a number of options were suggested as more moderate alternatives to the Jackson version of the amendment, Jackson's political savvy and his staff's organizational efforts were very effective in heading them off (Stern, 1979; Caldwell, 1981). On January 3, 1975, President Ford signed the Trade Reform Act (PL 93-618).

The Soviet reaction to the passage of the Jackson-Vanik amendment, and an additional amendment introduced by Senator Adlai Stevenson restricting Export-Import Bank credit to the Soviet Union, was swift. Arguing that they "categorically reject as inadmissable any attempts, from whomever they come, to interfere in affairs which are entirely within the internal competence of the Soviet state and do not concern anybody else" the Soviets nullified the Trade Agreement of 1974 (Caldwell, 1981, 16; Stern, 1979). Interestingly, however, by nullifying the agreement, rather than cancelling it the Soviets left open the option of signing it at some future date (Caldwell, 1981, 16).

Though the Trade Reform Act provides for resolutions of disapproval to block executive granting of MFN privileges, the Congress has exercised its prerogative with relatively weak resolve. Despite the fact that Congress has delegated less power to the executive in the area of trade than in other areas of foreign policy, it has been willing to allow the president considerable latitude in the extension of MFN status. The fervor which Jackson was able to create in order to pass the Jackson-Vanik amendment in the first place did not carry over into subsequent debates over MFN policy. In most of these cases there was little pressure for action from constituents, and thus representatives lacked the electoral motivation to expend political capital as well as the time and effort to take on the administration.

There had, of course, been points of debate, particularly over waivers for Romania which was extended MFN status in 1975 in order to encourage its independence from the Soviet Union (Kissinger, 1979). Yet of the 11 resolutions of disapproval introduced with respect to Romania between 1976 and 1986 none was reported out of the committee in the Senate. Of those which were reported out of committee in the House most were reported unfavorably. No resolutions of disapproval were ever passed by either chamber.

Poland, originally exempted from the broad denial of MFN status to communist countries, lost its trade status in 1982. Reacting to the imposition of martial law and the outlawing of the Solidarity trade union, President Reagan indefinitely suspended Poland's MFN status. (To justify this move, however, Reagan argued that Poland had not lived up to its commitments under GATT). Congress supported this move, though congressional concurrence was not needed for suspension. Poland did not regain its MFN status again until February 1987 (Pregelj, 1990a; *CQ Almanac*, 1982, 163).

On June 2, 1982, President Reagan waived Section 402 of the Trade Act of 1974 to renew waivers for China, Hungary and Romania. Hungary was extended MFN status in 1978 and China in 1980. Complaining of the inclusion of Romania, whose record on emigration was worsening from a high of 4,000 Jews permitted to emigrate to Israel in 1973 to 1,012 in 1981, conservatives in the Senate introduced resolutions of disapproval in order to rescind the waiver (*CQ Almanac*, 1982, 142).

According to conservative Senator Jesse Helms (R-N.C.) an "education repayment tax" imposed by the Rumanian government on emigres would amount to $3,700 for persons with a high school education and $4,000 for each year of college education (*CQ Almanac*, 1983, 265). Arguing for the waiver, President Reagan told Congress that he had receive assurances from Rumanian President Nicolae Ceausescu that his government "will not create economic or procedural barriers to emigration" and would lift the education tax. This brought swift denunciation on the floor of the House from Representative Richard Schulze (R-Pa.) who was "appalled that we are so gullible as to believe that this government in Romania will keep its promises when in the past they have responded with only short-term improvements in their policies on emigration" (*CQ Almanac*, 1983, 265).

While rhetoric was sharp from some quarters, the commitment to action was on the whole weak. In the House the Ways and Means Committee negatively reported the resolutions pertaining to China and Hungary and the chamber voted to postpone action, effectively killing moves to disapprove all three waivers. Likewise, the Senate Finance Committee rejected a related resolution on Romania (*CQ Almanac*, 1983, 265). This episode would prove characteristic of congressional action on MFN waivers until 1989.

Despite the lack of electoral motivation for congressional action on MFN, the institutional question remained. The 1989 debate over continuation of MFN status to Hungary served as a platform for confrontation between Congress and the president concerning institutional power over trade agreements. Though both branches agreed that Hungary's continued liberalization of emigration policy and shifts toward free-market principles deserved reward through continued MFN status, the debate centered on the president's authority to extend such status.

The Jackson-Vanik amendment allows the president to extend waivers to communist countries for a period of one year and requires semi-annual reports to Congress evaluating that country's progress on freedom of emigration policy. Arguing that he needed economic and political leverage to encourage the liberalization of Eastern European states, President Bush submitted a waiver for Hungary for a period of five years in return for Hungarian enactment of legislation which would greatly liberalize its emigration policy (*CQ Weekly Report*, September 9, 1989, 2325).

Though the resolution for the Hungarian waiver (HR 1594) was reported out of the Ways and Means Committee with the full five year extension, in a move considered by supporters of the president to be "a slap in the face" the full chamber voted to accept an amendment from Ways and Means Committee Chair Dan Rostenkowski (D-Ill.) to reduce the extension to a period of three years (*CQ Weekly Report*, September 9, 1989, 2325). Recognizing the potential power which trade concessions hold for influencing the newly democratizing states of Eastern Europe the Congress was careful not to limit their own participation in the exercise of a major tool of U.S. foreign policy. The importance of this tool was made all the more clear October 24, 1990 when Congress approved a one-year grant of MFN status to Czechoslovakia, the first Eastern European country to be extended the trade agreement after the fall of the Berlin Wall (*CQ Weekly Report*, October 27, 1990, 3586).

While the authors of the Jackson-Vanik amendment were able to create a context in which representatives were inspired both electorally and institutionally to pass the measure, the lack of interest group pressure in subsequent cases of MFN renewal weakened the likelihood of significant congressional action. Institutional motivations to maintain a congressional voice in trade policy kept some members active in debates over MFN status, but was insufficient to mount any major challenges to executive policy. This would soon change as Tienanmen Square and Soviet tanks in the Baltics thrust MFN trade status into the national and international spotlight.

## China and the Soviet Union

The June 3-4 1989 massacre of pro-democracy students in Tienanmen Square by Chinese government soldiers sent shock waves through the United States. Revulsion over the government handling of the demonstrations and the ensuing executions of student protest leaders, despite pleas for leniency from the American government, was initially reflected in the actions of both the executive and Congress. On June 5, 1989, government-to-government sales and commercial exports of weapons were banned by the administration along with high level military exchanges. As the executions of protest leaders proceeded all high level exchanges between government officials were suspended (October 20). The administration announced that it would seek to postpone consideration of Chinese loan applications to international financial institutions, and order Immigration and Naturalization officials to give "sympathetic review" to requests by Chinese students and visitors to extend their stay in the United States for another year (*CQ Weekly Report*, June 10, 1989, 1411; Harrison, et al., 1990).

In Congress a flurry of legislation was introduced to codify and extend the administration sanctions. Among those bills were import sanctions including denial of MFN status and reduction of textile quotas (critical to China's economy), suspension of arms and satellite sales, and withdrawal of U.S. export credits, investment and financial assistance (*CQ Weekly Report*, June 10, 1989, 1411; *CQ Weekly Report*, June 24, 1989, 1564; Harrison et al, 1990).

Soon, however, the branches began to diverge, with the administration seeming to back off of enforcing even its own sanctions while the Congress sought stiffer penalties against China. In fact conservative Republicans took the lead in calling for greater sanctions, criticizing the President's actions as too weak (*CQ Weekly Report*, July 1,

1989, 1642). Warning of going too far in alienating China through punishment, Bush said at a White House news conference, "I understand the importance of the relationship with the Chinese people and with the government. It is in the interest of the United States to have good relations" with China. Bush refused congressional pressure to recall U.S. ambassador James Lilley for "consultations" (*CQ Weekly Report,* June 10, 1989, 1411).

Administration back-sliding on sanctions against China undermined confidence in their sincerity. As a team of Congressional Research Service scholars note, "Officially, all the sanctions mentioned above remain in effect. However, the actual current state of U.S. activities in China is somewhat more complex..." (Harrison, et al., 1990, 2).

Specifically, the State Department on July 7, 1989, waived the suspension of military sales to allow the sale of 4 Boeing 757-200 commercial jets whose navigation systems have potential for military use; in October the administration allowed continued cooperation between U.S. and Chinese engineers to upgrade China's F-8 fighter jets with U.S. avionics; bans on high level official talks between U.S. and Chinese diplomats were breached when Secretary of State James Baker met Chinese Foreign Minister Qian Qichen during the Paris Conference on Cambodia in late July and again in New York in September, and when National Security Advisor Brent Scowcroft and Deputy Secretary of State Lawrence Eagleburger met with Chinese officials in a highly publicized meeting in December. Finally, on December 19, 1989, the administration authorized export licenses for three U.S. communications satellites to be launched on Chinese launch vehicles despite congressional legislation prohibiting the licenses (Harrison, et al., 1990, 4).

Congress' institutional role in trade policy, combined with legislators' electoral motivation to act in concert with strong public opinion and policy concerns over human rights, inspired congressional action. The administration's reluctance to enforce the sanctions called for by Congress laid the potential for conflict. Unlike previous disagreements over MFN, the high profile of the massacre in Tienanmen Square created strong and cohesive public opinion. Through policy convictions and public support Congress gained the will to oppose the president. The question now was how best to make that opposition effective in the formulation of U.S. policy. The answer reveals the true impact of the *Chadha* decision on MFN policy.

The first major showdown over U.S. policy toward China in the wake of Tienanmen centered on the issue of immigration extensions for Chinese students. In spite of administration objections, legislation was offered in both the House (HR 2929, HR 2712) and Senate (S 358) to extend visa terms for Chinese students afraid of persecution in China should they be forced to return (*CQ Weekly Report*, July 22, 1989). Because of Chinese government objections to the legislation, the Bush Administration lobbied against passage, arguing that a less formal presidential directive would accomplish the same goal and that students would not be forced to return against their will. In a vote that was seen as a "direct rebuke" to the administration the Senate passed S 358 (97-0) with Republican Minority Leader Robert Dole (R-Kan.) cosponsoring the legislation (*CQ Weekly Report*, July 15, 1989, 1787). The House passed its companion measure by voice vote. The protective legislation was estimated to affect approximately 40,000 Chinese students in this country (*CQ Weekly Report*, August 5, 1989, 2049). The final legislation, which reconciled minor differences between the House and Senate versions, (HR 2712) the Emergency Chinese Immigration Relief Act of 1989, was passed unanimously (403-0) in the House and by voice vote in the Senate (*CQ Weekly Report*, December 2, 1989, 3316).

In spite of such overwhelming bipartisan congressional support, the president vetoed the bill. In his veto message he argued, although "I share the objectives of the overwhelming majority in the Congress who passed this legislation....My actions today accomplish the laudable objectives of the Congress in passing H.R. 2712 while preserving my ability to manage foreign affairs" (Bush, 1989).

He further argued that by administratively, rather than legislatively, implementing a presidential directive protecting Chinese students until January 1, 1994, his actions provided the same protection as the congressional measure without irreparably damaging future relations with the Chinese whom he felt confident would "return to the policy of reform pursued before June 3" (Bush, 1989).

The immediate and angry reaction from Congress included charges that the president was "kowtowing to Beijing" (*CQ Weekly Report*, December 2, 1989, 3316). On January 25 the House voted over-whelmingly to override the veto (390-25). The president's veto was sustained, however, in the Senate by four votes (62-37). All of those voting to sustain the veto were Republicans (Bush, 1989).

Even the Republican leaders in the Senate who had orchestrated the vote to sustain the president's veto admitted that their commitment was to Bush politically rather than his China policy. "It's not about China policy," claimed Senate Minority Leader Dole. "It's American politics." Bush, however, chose to interpret the victory as a policy endorsement. "(I)t gives me the confidence that I'm going to go forward the way that I think is correct here [on China policy]" (*CQ Weekly Report*, January 27, 1990, 245). Thus, tensions ran high between Congress and the president contributing to another conflict developing simultaneously over U.S. policy toward China: whether to waive restrictions for MFN status.

The week before the Tienanmen massacre President Bush had extended China's waiver for MFN status. With no forewarning of the upcoming events, the waiver met little opposition in Congress. When the tanks rolled into Tienanmen Square, however, Congress immediately called upon the president to, among other sanctions, rescind MFN status for China (*CQ Weekly Report*, June 24, 1989, 1564). Sticking to his conviction that the United States could maintain greater leverage over China by keeping trade relations alive, Bush refused. China's MFN status, extended for another year, would not run out again until June 3, 1991, the one-year anniversary of Tienanmen.

During this same period peaceful revolutions were sweeping Eastern Europe and Gorbachev's glasnost policies were having dramatic effects in the Soviet Union. In order to encourage continued reforms and fortify Gorbachev against his conservative opponents President Bush, in trade talks with the Soviets, had suggested extending MFN status to that country. Threats of Soviet military intervention to quell nationalist separatist movements in the Baltic States, particularly Lithuania, raised calls from Congress to tie any agreement to grant MFN status to Gorbachev's handling of the situation.

With both the China and Soviet MFN status questions looming, Congress took a serious look at its ability to block such initiatives should policy disagreements between the president and Congress come to loggerheads. Until 1983 Congress had been able to block MFN waivers by either one-house veto or concurrent resolution. In the aftermath of the *Chadha* decision, Congress' leverage was in question. Having never seriously threatened an executive waiver in the wake of the Court's decision, the Jackson-Vanik amendment stood as written, constitutionally dubious legislative vetoes and all. In anticipation of the upcoming battles over China and the Soviet Union, therefore, Congress included in Section 132 of the Customs and Trade Act of 1990 (PL 101-382) provisions to replace the legislative vetoes in the Jackson-Vanik amendment with joint resolutions of disapproval (*CQ Weekly Report*, April 28, 1990, 1249). The bill was signed into law August 20, 1990 (Pregelj, 1990b, 1-3).

The clash over the 1990-91 renewal of MFN for China erupted on May 24, 1990, when Bush announced his decision to once again grant that country a waiver of trade restrictions. Reaction was quick in both chambers against the grant, as even Republican lawmakers such as New York's Alfonse D'Amato called Bush's policy "a short-sighted accommodation with a blood stained and discredited regime" (*CQ Weekly Report*, May 26, 1990, 1639).

Numerous bills and amendments were introduced which would have either cancelled China's MFN status immediately or imposed severe restrictions on the next year's MFN waiver. The House Ways and Means Committee favorably reported legislation introduced by Representative Don Pease (D-Ohio) tying extension of MFN status to China beyond June 1991 to "significant" improvements in China's human rights record (*CQ Weekly Report*, July 14, 1990, 2200; *CQ Weekly Report*, July 21, 1990, 2288). This legislation would, for the first time, extend the Jackson-Vanik requirements beyond emigration to human rights. In the Senate, Majority Leader George Mitchell (D-Maine) and 21 co-sponsors introduced stiffer legislation which would revoke MFN immediately, restoring it only when the president certified even greater gains in human rights in China than the House bill required (*CQ Weekly Report*, July 21, 1990, 2288).

The administration's steadfast refusal to heed congressional sentiment appeared to radicalize the House. On October 18, when the time came to vote, the House rallied to pass legislation equally as stiff as the Mitchell bill. By a vote of 247-174 the House passed a bill introduced by Gerald Solomon (R-N.Y.) (H.J. Res 647) disapproving Bush's waiver for China. In addition, by a vote of 384-30 the chamber passed legislation introduced by Nancy Pelosi (D-Calif.) stiffening the standards which China would have to meet in the future (under Jackson-Vanik) to qualify for presidential certification of adequately improved human rights behavior (*CQ Weekly Report*, October 20, 1990).

The vote in the House was more symbolic than substantive, however, as the congressional session recessed before the Senate was able to act on the Mitchell-proposed companion legislation. In any event, the message was clear to the president that dissatisfaction within Congress was substantial over the issue of MFN to China. Instead of compromising behind the scenes, the conflict between the president and Congress was in full public view.

In July, 1991 Bush again announced his intention to extend China's MFN status, and again Congress went into an uproar. Though the administration proposed a multi-year extension, both the House and Senate passed legislation limiting continued MFN status to one year with further extensions conditional upon human rights improvements and the cessation of Chinese arms sales to the Middle East. Though the congressional action constitutes a major rebuff to Bush, the Senate is expected to sustain the president's veto which will inevitably follow.

Why, one might ask, does Congress not simply cut off China's MFN status completely? Legislators have demonstrated both the motivation and the will to oppose the president on this issue, so why go only part way? The answer may well lie more in cross-pressures within legislators' constituencies than in any desire to compromise with the president.

Congress is often considered to reflect the short-term passions of public opinion in the United States. In the case of the Tienanmen Square killings, this would certainly appear to have been the case. There are, however, longer-term considerations which moderate congressional reactions and calls for maximum sanctions or absolute denial of MFN to China. While members' broad (mass public) constituency clearly called for a strong reaction to the brutal crackdown on student protestors in Tienanmen Square, the more specialized business community pressed for more moderate sanctions which would not completely undermine the significant investments of U.S. business interests in China.

China is the tenth largest trading partner to the United States. In 1989 the United States exported $5.8 billion worth of goods to China and imported $18 billion (U.S. Department of Commerce figures; Harrison et.al., 1990, 8). U.S. investment in China is estimated to be $3.5 billion, or 12% of total foreign investment. Should the United States deny it MFN status, the Chinese government announced in May, 1990, that it would reciprocate by cutting off purchases of U.S. goods (*CQ Weekly Report*, June 9, 1990, 1775). The bulk of U.S. exports to China consist of industrial supplies, capital goods and food and beverages (U.S. Department of Commerce; Harrison et. al., 1990, 10). Several powerful U.S. companies, including Boeing Co. and McDonnell Douglas Corp. have major contracts to provide aircraft and technology to the Chinese. The suspension of Chinese imports of these products would clearly damage U.S. business interests. In fact, a report prepared by specialists at the Congressional Research Service determined that since other members of the General Agreement on Tariffs and Trade (GATT) and the Coordinating Committee on Multilateral Export Controls (CoCom) trading bloc--consisting of the U.S., Japan, and most NATO countries--did not appear inclined to join in trade sanctions against China, "U.S. business would bear the brunt of unilateral sanctions" (Harrison, et.al., 1990, 18).

An even greater burden of denying MFN status, however, may well fall upon consumers within the United States. The vast majority of U.S. imports from China are consumer goods, particularly clothing ($698.1 million) and toys ($642.2 million) (U.S. Department of Commerce; *CQ Weekly Report*, June 9, 1990, 1775). Should MFN status be denied, the U.S. Department of Commerce estimates that the tariff on toys, now at 6.8%, would rise to 70% while that on clothing would rise from 6% to 60% (*CQ Weekly Report*, June 9, 1990, 1775). MFN status is therefore of mutual benefit to both the United States and China, and by its denial we may well end up shooting ourselves in the pocketbook.

Thus, members of Congress have had to balance the demands of an impassioned mass public whose mobilization is likely to be short-term with those of a more specialized constituency whose interests are certain to be a longer-term, recurrent consideration. Whether a Congress with the capacity to unilaterally deny China MFN status, via legislative veto, would have actually done so is therefore open to debate. This question aside, however, the administration's flagrant disregard of congressional sentiment over the issue led Congress not only to formally implement legislation reinstating some degree of leverage over policy (the Customs and Trade Act) but also served to rally support behind drastic and confrontational legislation against China in the effort to make itself heard. As Republican Representative William Broomfield (Mich.), ranking minority member of the Foreign Affairs Committee argued, stiffer congressional legislation "is not an attempt to undercut (the president)....It simply recognizes that Congress has a role in stating broad policy directions" (*CQ Weekly Report*, July 1, 1989, 1642).

That same sentiment prevailed on the issue of MFN to the Soviet Union. President Bush reached a tentative trade accord with the Soviet Union on May 26, 1990, which included the granting of MFN status (Pregelj, 1989; *CQ Weekly Report*, April 28, 1990, 1249). The accord was signed by both parties June 1. But Congress was not to be steamrolled. If the president would not heed congressional sentiment over the situation in Lithuania, and could not be compelled to consult more seriously with Congress through the threat of a legislative veto, then direct legislation was an effective alternative. As *Congressional Quarterly* reporter John Cranford observed,

> the ink was barely dry on the Soviet trade agreement when the House voted overwhelmingly June 6 to bar new high-technology exports to the Soviet Union until the Soviet government stops using economic coercion against Lithuania and begins serious negotiations to allow the republic's independence (*CQ Weekly Report*, June 9, 1990, 1773).

The vote was 390-24, signalling the president of serious confrontation ahead over the U.S.-Soviet trade agreement. In the face of obvious congressional opposition in both the House and Senate, Bush decided to refrain from sending Congress the trade agreement until new emigration practices are codified in Soviet law.

The dissolution of the Soviet Union, of course, renders the issue moot. Debates over the extension of MFN status to the independent republics will likely revolve around similar considerations, however, and will certainly be seen as an important element of U.S. foreign policy toward the new states. It would appear that William Archey, International Vice President of the U.S. Chamber of Commerce had a point when he argued, "Trade is never going to be for its own sake. It's always going to be in some geopolitical context" (*CQ Weekly Report*, June 9, 1990, 1773).

## MFN Policy: The Politics and Structure
## of Interbranch Relations

The case of MFN trade status provides an illustration of the potentially changing nature of issues. Those which under one set of circumstances appear to hold relatively little potential for conflict between the branches may in fact prove highly contentious when the context in which they are framed changes. In the case of MFN, changes in the international context of the debate had strong repercussions within the United States, altering the political and domestic considerations which members of Congress confronted. Where at one time the extension of MFN status lacked a strong constituency basis for confronting the president (particularly over Romania, Hungary or China), suddenly there was a highly impassioned mass constituency to consider. Not only did members have an institutional motivation for participating in U.S. trade policy, but they also had a strong electoral motivation to be seen as acting in the moral crusade against brutal human rights violations in China and the Soviet Union. Though these motivations were tempered by the longer term interests of the business community (the desire not to irreparably damage the mutually beneficial openings between the U.S. and China) and the strong support for Gorbachev's reforms in the Soviet Union, they were sufficient to catalyze Congress into action on an issue which for over a decade had been left mainly to the discretion of the executive.

The conflict arose not strictly because of congressional action on the issue of MFN, but because of executive propriety over the issue. The administration's refusal to significantly compromise with Congress, particularly over the extension of visas for Chinese students and its reversal on enforcing the already insufficient sanctions against China, gave Congress the choice of either backing down on the issue or taking measures to compel serious consideration of its views. In the case of China, hearings, direct counter-legislation and the threat of resolutions of disapproval were the chosen tactics. In contrast to the more behind-the-scenes consultation and compromise characteristic of executive efforts to avoid a legislative veto threat, these disagreements were played out in full public (both domestic and international) view.

In the period between the passage of the Jackson-Vanik amendment and 1989 there was very little electoral motivation for members to act with any decisiveness to counter executive waivers of MFN. Acting on institutional motivations in the wake of *Chadha*, legislators did introduce bills and resolutions opposing executive actions concerning MFN waivers, but did not seriously threaten initiatives. With the changes in the international context of the issue, particularly in relation to China and the Soviet Union, however, strong public opinion and commitments to human rights catalyzed congressional action. Despite the fact that there was significant room for overlap between the administration and congressional positions on the issue of MFN to China and the Soviet Union (neither the majority of congressional members, particularly in the House, nor the executive really wanted to irrevocably rescind China's trade status or jeopardize Gorbachev's stability in the Soviet Union) the president's refusal to make satisfactory overtures of consultation and compromise drove members of Congress to take a more radical stance than even their own original positions would seem to have warranted. Lacking the legislative veto with which Congress might have seriously threatened to unilaterally kill the president's trade agreements, the executive had little incentive to make any serious attempts to modify his initiatives.

The alternatives left to the Congress, formally codified in the Trade and Customs Act changing the legislative vetoes to joint resolutions of disapproval, were mechanisms which, by their nature, were higher profile and increase the likelihood of conflict. Direct counter-legislation provides Congress with a powerful mechanism to affect policy but is seen as a "direct rebuke" to the president. Moreover, this legislation is subject to presidential veto and the inevitable publicity which accompanies such obvious confrontations between legislature and executive. Joint resolutions of disapproval, likewise, are unquestionably a public denunciation of presidential policy. Even in the event of a presidential veto and the inability to override, merely the passage of the initial disapproval leaves scars on the interbranch relationship and raises a flag in the international (and domestic) community of dissention among the top levels of government in the United States. Confidence in the ability to carry out agreements is indispensable to the president's credibility in the international arena. High profile confrontations, such as those which have occurred over China and the Soviet Union, can do serious damage not only to present but to future trade negotiations. They send conflicting signals concerning the U.S. commitment to human rights as well as trade relationships, and further undermine the international impression of a coherent and stable American foreign policy.

# 7

---

# Congressional Involvement When It Doesn't Play in Peoria: Nuclear Nonproliferation Policy

The formulation of nuclear nonproliferation policy in the U.S. is representative of a category of foreign policy issues which inspire only occasional interbranch controversy: strategic non-salient issues. In terms relative to strategic-salient or intermestic issues, strategic non-salient issues are marked by only moderate or occasional conflict between Congress and the executive. As with strategic-salient issues, strategic non-salient issues involve the international balance of power. In the case of nuclear capabilities, for example, the threat of nuclear retaliation in regional or global hostilities is fundamental to international relations and the leverage which nations can wield against one another.

Strategic non-salient issues lack the same potential for conflict, however, because they do not inspire the same degree of constituent pressure on legislators to firmly oppose the president in cases of policy disagreement. Thus, while the issue at hand may sustain an institutional motivation to participate in policy making, the lack of reelection or policy entrepreneurial rewards undermines electoral motivation. The costs of opposing the president in this area of foreign policy appear to outweigh the gains to be made, and so legislators remain relatively deferential. In terms of our theoretical framework, then, the flow of opposition most often ends at congressional assertion.

On occasion, however, an event inspires sufficient concern, both in the public and among legislators, to catalyze congressional assertion. In these instances of policy disagreement, legislators threatened the use of the legislative veto to influence policy, but often lacked the ultimate congressional will to follow through on the threat. In the aftermath of

*Chadha* the same weak resolve holds true for threatened joint resolutions of disapproval.

Two primary reasons account for this. First, given the overall non-salient nature of the issue, the short-term mobilization in public opinion which may inspire congressional assertion on policy is unlikely to be sustained for the period of time it takes to go through the process of disapproval. Congress is hesitant to kill an executive policy when public support is ephemeral. Second, and relatedly, because public support is likely to be short-lived, Congress does not want to take ultimate responsibility for strategic policy. International power balance is an inherently difficult and quixotic policy area. Congress is more inclined to let the president take the initiative, and the knocks, for the formulation of U.S. strategic policy.

Examining the case of nuclear nonproliferation policy will help to illustrate the characteristics of interbranch relations on strategic-nonsalient issues. By demonstrating why interbranch conflict is less likely to occur, the case study also provides the foundation for the conclusion that the *Chadha* decision has had only moderate impact on congressional-executive relations in this policy area. Indeed, though a qualitative analysis can highlight individual instances in which conflict has arisen, that impact has not led to a sustained pattern in the quantitative measure of conflict. In the absence of serious conflict, there is less need for a statutory mechanism to resolve interbranch disputes. Despite the loss of the legislative veto the policy process in strategic non-salient issues is still marked by relatively feeble resolve on the part of the legislature.

## Determining the Potential for Conflict

In contrast to arms sales to the Middle East or MFN trade status, nuclear non-proliferation policy illustrates a case conducive to only moderate or occasional conflict between the executive and legislative branches. A specific look at the factors which affect congressional assertion over nonproliferation policy reveals why.

### Institutional Motives for Congressional Action

Given the serious potential for international instability born of uncontrolled proliferation of nuclear materials and technology, coupled with Congress' constitutional role in regulating trade with other countries, the institutional incentive for congressional involvement is clear. In the aftermath of World War II disputes over nuclear capabilities, their regulation and containment, have been pivotal in international relations. As the chronology of U.S. nuclear policy to follow makes clear, Congress has always taken an active interest in legislation safeguarding the use of nuclear technology and weaponry.

Still, the regulation of nuclear capabilities is an issue unique to the postwar period. It is clearly not an issue which the Framers of the Constitution anticipated, though it illustrates the wisdom of building flexibility into the document for the handling of "national exigencies" which were "impossible to foresee or define" (Hamilton, Federalist 23, 1787). The Constitution does not spell out who is to control weapons of mass destruction. Moreover, the inherent crisis aspect of nuclear weapons colors the entire debate (even over peaceful uses of nuclear technology) and underpins arguments favoring executive flexibility in policy making.

Nuclear nonproliferation is a child of World War II, a product (and cause) of the U.S.' superpower status. Having arisen at a time when presidential leadership in foreign policy was the norm, despite congressional involvement in formulating policy, the country has ultimately looked to the executive for policy governing the use and restriction of nuclear weapons. The image of the one man with his finger on "the button" is a powerful one.

So, while Congress clearly has an institutional motive to participate in policy regulating nuclear weapons and technology based upon its delegated powers over interstate commerce, war powers, and the making of laws which are "necessary and proper" to the execution of all governmental powers, legislators continually demonstrate trepidation at taking over policy making in so momentous an arena.

## *Electoral Motives for Congressional Action*

The electoral motivation for legislators to become involved in this issue has varied over the course of the last two decades. During the 1970s India's test explosion of a nuclear bomb, and reports of agreements between industrialized and Third World countries for transfer of nuclear materials and technology, galvanized and already growing "no nukes" branch of the environmental movement in the United States. Significant pressure was brought to bear on individual legislators to take an active stand on nuclear proliferation issues, leading to a great deal of legislation in the mid-1970s.

As the environmental movement has lost some steam in the 1980s, however, and no Less Developed Countries have publicly tested nuclear devices, the pressure for congressional action has subsided. Focus on nuclear proliferation issues dwindled in the 1980s to a small group of dedicated legislators who at times were able to muster support for nonproliferation policy. Generally the issue fell out of the limelight.

Lacking constituency pressure, legislators have had little electoral incentive to expend a significant amount of time or effort on nonproliferation issues. As one Senate staffer lamented,

> Unfortunately, nonproliferation doesn't really have a local element to it....No American is happy about the thought of weapons of mass destruction spreading around the world, however, it is a threat which is remote, abstract, it isn't real....So there's not a lot of pressure being put on Congress to do something about the proliferation threat.

As policy entrepreneurs, a few member of Congress have found the issue of nuclear nonproliferation attractive. Senator Glenn (D-Ohio), for example, has been a primary spokesperson for enforcement of U.S. and international nonproliferation agreements. But while the efforts of a few keep the issue alive, and occasionally on the legislative agenda, they have had only meager success in galvanizing the support of their colleagues.

Despite institutional motives to participate in policy formulation, then, the lack of electoral motivation on the part of the majority of legislators has kept congressional assertion to a minimum.

### Presidential Policy Position and Congressional Will to Act

On those occasions when Congress has become involved in nonproliferation policy, it has often been either in the absence of strong executive action or when congressional and executive policy preferences coincide. In cases of policy disagreement, however, Congress has lacked the will to use the full range of its statutory tools to oppose the executive.

During the Nixon and Ford Administrations, Congress felt that executive policy was much too lax, leading to a strong congressional legislative initiative. This coincided with the height of pressure from the environmental movement for congressional restrictions on nuclear proliferation. In 1976 and 1977 the Symington and Glenn amendments to the Foreign Assistance Act of 1961 were passed. The amendments required a mandatory cutoff of U.S. aid to countries which exported or imported nuclear reprocessing or enrichment facilities unless that country accepted and adhered to International Atomic Energy Agency (IAEA) safeguards (Cassidy, 1989). Both amendments included legislative vetoes for congressional oversight.

During the early Carter Administration, by contrast, the initiative for nonproliferation policy shifted to the executive. "In 1977 President Carter preempted the non-proliferation issue by proposing his own strong policy statement and draft legislation" (Donnelly, 1983b, 10). At this point the views of the executive largely coincided with those of congressional adherents to nonproliferation policy, making for smooth and cooperative relations between the branches on the issue.

This cooperative relationship became strained by the end of the Carter Administration. Congressional advocates of strict nonproliferation policy charged that administration priorities favored short-term foreign policy considerations over the serious enforcement of long-term nonproliferation policy (Baker, 1984). But despite some rhetoric criticizing the administration, Congress made little serious effort to influence policy.

The coming of the Reagan Administration fortified congressional discontent with executive policy and, among those members active on the issue, a perceived need to reinforce legislative restrictions. The Reagan Administration espoused a "new realism" in U.S. nonproliferation policy (Donnelly, 1983b, 11). As a tool of foreign policy, they argued, nuclear materials and technology should be used to reward strong allies and stable recipient countries. The administration viewed German and French suppliers of nuclear materials and technology as undermining American leverage abroad and argued for reestablishing the United States as a "reliable supplier." This view conflicted with the prevailing sentiment in Congress that supply of nuclear materials should be unrelated to politics or international relations, but should rest on issues of security, safety, and assurances of non-military domestic use.

During the early Reagan Administration Congress fortified the Glenn and Symington amendments through the International Security and Development Cooperation Act of 1981 which added legislative veto provisions by concurrent resolution and a separate subsection on the testing of nuclear devices (Donnelly, 1983c, 2; Cassidy, 1989, 694). But strengthening the legislation was ineffectual without the will to enforce it. Though rhetoric was sharp, congressional threats were largely hollow as the administration continued to evade and disregard legislative restrictions.

Congress did impose report-and-wait requirements on the executive but failed to ultimately kill controversial transfers of nuclear materials and technology. The national security implications of nonproliferation policy, the executive access to classified information, lack of public interest, and congressional reluctance to take responsibility for such a sensitive policy area all weighed against serious congressional opposition.

The result has been relatively unfettered executive policy making regardless of congressional access to the legislative veto.

## Conflict Between the Branches

The 1983 *Chadha* decision did concern a number of members interested in nonproliferation policy, particularly given the Reagan Administration stance on the issue. As will be seen, the decision has negatively affected Congress' ability to influence nonproliferation policy, though its impact is mitigated by the relatively weak motivation of members to become heavily involved in the issue. In the wake of the *Chadha* decision "the executive branch relaxed the interpretation of the statutory policies embodied by the nonproliferation legislation" (Clark, 1986, 901) and took fairly flagrant liberties with sales of nuclear materials abroad. In fact the Reagan Administration's reluctance to even comply with reporting requirements inspired several members of Congress to bring suit against the president and several administration officials (*Cranston v. Reagan*) to get a judicial determination on whether export agreements could contain advance consent provisions[9] (Clark, 1986, fn.16).

Episodes such as these reveal that Congress is not willing to totally resign itself to the executive on the issue of nuclear nonproliferation. As the legislative chronology to follow shows, at times legislators have been quite vocal in opposition to specific proposals to export nuclear materials or to circumvent legislative restrictions.

In terms of overall conflict, however, the loss of the legislative veto has had only moderate impact on conflict between the branches. Lacking the will to enforce the veto in the first place, the impact of the *Chadha* decision has had little effect on congressional policy participation. Though Congress has continued to pass legislation to restrict the proliferation of nuclear materials and technology, it has been relatively weak in its enforcement.

Figure 7.1 presents the number of bills and resolutions introduced in opposition to the president over the issue of nuclear nonproliferation policy as a percentage of all bills and resolutions introduced from the 95th to 101st Congresses. The data support the argument presented here that although there has been some opposition expressed through congressional legislation, the loss of the legislative veto in the 98th Congress has had little discernible effect on the pattern of bills and resolutions introduced. As expected, the *Chadha* decision has not led to greater interbranch conflict in this issue area.

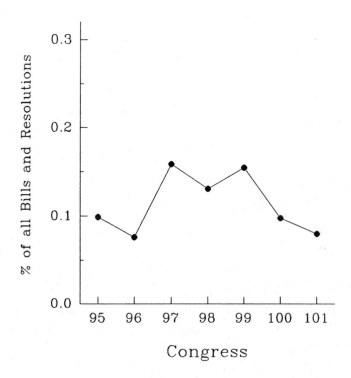

FIGURE 7.1    Bills and Resolutions: Nuclear Nonproliferation (95th-101st Congress).

A detailed examination of the formulation of U.S. nonproliferation policy and interbranch relations on the issue will help to provide foundation for this conclusion.

### Nonproliferation Policy and
### Executive-Legislative Relations

In the aftermath of World War II U.S. dominance in the world of nuclear weapons thrust the issue of nuclear competition and proliferation onto the legislative agenda.  From the beginning, Congress took steps to ensure its participation in the nuclear policy of the country. The 1946 Atomic Energy Act provided for the creation of the Atomic Energy Commission, an independent agency within the executive branch responsible for development and implementation of U.S. nuclear policy. Until this time the United States had been the sole possessor of nuclear weapons and thus viewed its role as protecting the secrecy of nuclear technology.

By 1949, however, the Soviet Union had successfully tested its own nuclear device, followed in 1953 by Great Britain (Cassidy, 1989, 690). In 1954, the Eisenhower Administration, marking a shift in U.S. policy toward "Atoms for Peace," proposed an amendment to the Atomic Energy Act of 1946 permitting limited exchanges of technology and data with other countries. The resulting legislation, the Atomic Energy Act of 1954, granted executive authority to such limited exchanges on the condition that the countries accept safeguards and give assurances that the materials would be used solely for domestic purposes. The act further required that the executive submit exchange agreements to Congress for review (Public Law No. 83-703, 68 Stat. 919 [1954]).

In 1968 the United Nations General Assembly proposed an international agreement to control the spread of nuclear capabilities. The end product of its efforts was the 1969 Treaty on the Non-Proliferation of Nuclear Weapons (NPT) which to date has 135 signatory nations. The treaty divides countries into "nuclear weapons states" to denote those which had detonated a nuclear device prior to 1967 and "non-nuclear states" for the remainder. Nations a party to this treaty agree not to manufacture or receive nuclear explosives, to accept IAEA safeguards on all peaceful nuclear activities, not to assist non-weapons states in obtaining nuclear arms, not to export nuclear materials to non-weapons states except under IAEA safeguards, to share peaceful nuclear technology, and agree to pursue negotiations in good faith to end the nuclear arms race and achieve nuclear disarmament under international control (Spector, 1988, 459).

Though a number of weapons and non-weapons states signed the NPT, not all agreed. Of greatest concern among the non-treaty countries have been China and France (both of whom are weapons states), and India, Israel, Pakistan, South Africa, Argentina and Brazil. (China and France have only recently agreed "in principle" to sign the NPT (*Los Angeles Times*, August 11, 1991, A1.) Iraq is a signatory to the treaty but has been criticized recently for covertly undermining the IAEA safeguards process. India, Argentina and Brazil have declared the treaty to be discriminatory to non-weapons states, barring them from acquiring nuclear capabilities while allowing weapons states to retain their nuclear devices and exempting the United States, Soviet Union and Britain from IAEA safeguard regulations (*CQ Weekly Report*, July 11, 1981, 1227). Thus while Argentina and Brazil have agreed to sign the Tlateloco Treaty for nuclear non-proliferation in Latin America (1967) all three refuse to become adherents to the NPT (*Los Angeles Times*, November 28, 1990).

In 1974 a number of events came together to heighten congressional concern over U.S. nonproliferation policy and add fuel to the growing anti-nuclear wing of the environmental movement. The most startling event was India's successful testing of its own nuclear device in that year. Suddenly the illusion that nuclear capability was limited to a few industrialized nations was shattered, and the prospect of Third World nations acquiring (either overtly or covertly) the wherewithal to make their own nuclear devices became a reality. In addition, news of French agreements to supply South Korea and Pakistan with reprocessing plants, and a German contract to supply Brazil with a "complete nuclear industry including, ultimately, facilities for reprocessing and enrichment" (Donnelly, 1983b, 9) raised fears of uncontrolled proliferation of nuclear capabilities throughout the world.

On June 25, 1974, the House Foreign Affairs Committee held hearings to evaluate President Nixon's announced agreements for nuclear cooperation with Egypt and Israel. These were followed on July 12, 1974, by hearings in the Committee on Banking, Housing and Urban Affairs to evaluate overall controls on U.S. exports of nuclear materials and technology. Senator Adlai Stevenson (D-Ill.) represented prevailing congressional fears over administration policy, arguing,

> At the present time, the United States does not have a coherent nuclear policy--unless it is to promote the indiscriminate sale of nuclear facilities abroad. Nor does it have a coherent procedure for controlling nuclear exports....So the nation faces the growing danger of nuclear holocaust, international blackmail and the poisoning of the atmosphere (cited in Donnelly, 1989b, 5).

Compounding this conflict was the fact that executive jurisdiction over proliferation policy had shifted from the Atomic Energy Commission (AEC) in 1974 due to charges of conflicts of interest between the commission's dual roles of development and regulation of nuclear power. As Donnelly explains,

> these major organizational changes put control over exports of nuclear plant, equipment and materials into the hands of the Nuclear Regulatory Commission (NRC) but left control over technical assistance and technology transfer...in the Department of Energy (DOE). While these changes may have resolved the problem of conflict of interest over

nuclear development and nuclear safety, they unwittingly opened the way for today's situation wherein the responsibilities of the State Department combine both its dominant foreign policy functions with that of development and carrying out of U.S. non-proliferation policy. From the standpoint of those who would prefer U.S. non-proliferation policy to be insulated from considerations of foreign policy and international relations, this evolution may simply have swapped one conflict of interest for another (Donnelly, 1983a, 3).

Congressional concern over strengthening U.S. non-proliferation policy took legislative form in two important amendments to the Foreign Assistance Act of 1961. The Symington Amendment, passed in 1976 (PL 94-329), bars aid to nations which export or import uranium enrichment technology or materials without agreeing to proper IAEA safeguards. The Glenn Amendment, passed in 1977 (PL 95-92) bars aid to non-treaty nations who export or import nuclear reprocessing equipment or materials, or to any nation that detonates a nuclear device. Each of these amendments included waiver provisions whereby the president could petition to have the restrictions lifted, though these waivers were subject to legislative veto by concurrent resolution.

Such congressional initiatives on nonproliferation policy were paralleled by proposals coming from the Carter Administration. By 1977 U.S. nuclear exports accounted for 90 percent of atomic fuel used by non-communist countries around the world (*CQ Almanac*, 1977, 400). Recognizing the crucial role this implied for both U.S. domestic fuel and export policy Carter renounced the use of plutonium by the United States (citing the danger that the spent fuel could be reprocessed to make nuclear weapons) and called for strict legislation guiding export of nuclear materials and technology.    Compromises made between administration policy proposals and congressional legislative initiatives would culminate in the Nuclear Non-Proliferation Act (NNPA) of 1978.

The NNPA, the high water mark of American nonproliferation policy, serves as an illustrative example of executive-legislative codetermination of U.S. foreign policy. Though the goals of the Carter Administration and congressional advocates of nuclear proliferation restrictions coincided, there remained disputes over the details of the ensuing legislation. In the end, both the administration and Congress prevailed in a number of demands while acquiescing on others (Baker, 1984; Cassidy, 1989). The administration, for example, won concessions on: timely warning standards (arguing that congressional restrictions on early warning of diversion of nuclear materials were unrealistic given the state of technology at the time and unduly tied the president's hands in international negotiations); exemptions for the European Atomic Energy

Community (Euroatom); clarification of approval requirements for customer nations' storage facilities; addition of the Secretary of Defense to the list of those consulted on technology transfers; and clarification of amounts of weapons-grade nuclear materials subject to congressional notification requirements before transfer abroad (*CQ Almanac*, 1977, 401).

Though Congress was willing to concede to the executive on the aforementioned points, it maintained strong statutory control over exports through the inclusion of nine legislative veto provisions. The vetoes, all by concurrent resolution, covered multiple areas of the nonproliferation act, including international undertakings, agreements for reprocessing, storage of spent fuel (one covering American spent fuel, another covering foreign spent fuel to be stored in the United States), authorization of exports that do not meet NNPA criteria, authorization of exports that do not meet full scope safeguard criteria, presidential determinations concerning effects of agreements on recipient countries' nuclear capabilities and on U.S. nonproliferation policy, and agreements for cooperative ventures (P.L.95-242; see also Donnelly, 1983c, 2; Clark, 1986, fn. 60; *CQ Almanac*, 1978, 350-358; Collier, et.al., 1985, 11).

While Carter favored strong non-proliferation legislation he objected to the legislative veto provisions. In the end Carter signed the act saying,

> Although I still have reservations about the numerous provisions in this act which state that Congress may invalidate or approve executive branch action by concurrent resolution, I am signing it because of its overwhelming importance to our nonproliferation policy. I do wish to make clear, however, that by signing this act, I am not agreeing that the Congress can overturn authorized executive actions through procedures not provided in the Constitution (Carter, 1978, 502; for discussion see Schick, 1983, 177; and Donnelly, 1983c, 3).

That same year Carter found himself facing the first legislative veto threat over nonproliferation policy when he announced his intention to sell enriched nuclear fuel to India. Opposition to the sale came not only from members of Congress but also from the Nuclear Regulatory Commission which was split 2-2 on the sale (one seat on the commission was vacant at the time). The lukewarm reception which Carter's proposal received stemmed mainly from the fact that India had refused to accept international safeguards on its nuclear facilities. After intensive lobbying, including a trip to Capitol Hill by Indian Prime Minister Desai, the resolution to disapprove the sale was voted down in the House 181-227 (*CQ Almanac*, 1978, 371 and 466; Donnelly 1990a, 7). India got the nuclear fuel, and strict enforcement of the tough new nonproliferation laws had gotten off to a shaky start.

The greatest challenge to U.S. commitment to nonproliferation came in 1979 after clear indications that Pakistan had attempted to covertly acquire nuclear materials for its Kahuta enrichment plant. Initially, Congress and the president were in agreement on the need to enforce the Symington amendment to the Foreign Assistance Act of 1961 (Sec. 669) by cutting off aid to Pakistan. The Soviet invasion of Afghanistan later in 1979, however, significantly changed the picture. After eight months, without obtaining the cooperation of Congress, President Carter reversed himself, offering Pakistani President Zia ul-Haq $400 million, but his offer was dismissed by the Pakistani as "peanuts" (*CQ Almanac*, 1987, 168; Baker, 1984).

The settlement over Pakistan had left some bitter feelings in Congress over the general ability of the U.S. to enforce its strict nuclear export policy. Thus the stage was set for a battle when President Carter requested a waiver of the Glenn-Symington amendments for India, who had not accepted international safeguards on their nuclear facilities. Carter's proposal to sell nuclear fuel to India met strong hostility in the House and was defeated through a resolution of disapproval, 298-98.

Determined to save the sale, Carter focussed his lobbying efforts on the Senate. Two major factors helped his argument: first, as Baker argues, "for most Senators, the Indian nuclear fuel license was not a major issue; certainly, as a foreign policy concern it was subordinate to the ongoing hostage crisis in Iran and the Soviet intervention in Afghanistan" (Baker, 1984, 150).

Second, Carter made note of the fact that India had just announced in May 1980 a $1.6 billion deal with the U.S.S.R. for nuclear materials, strengthening the need for American cooperation with India in order to maintain its leverage there (Baker, 1984, 146). In the end, the proposal was saved in the Senate, though by a narrow margin of 48-46. Though Congress was unwilling to actually kill the president's initiative, the message was clear that dissatisfaction with half-hearted enforcement of export restrictions was strong (*CQ Weekly Report*, July 11, 1981, 1225).

The aid cutoff to Pakistan lasted until 1981 when the Reagan Administration requested some revisions to the Symington amendment to allow for aid to Pakistan. The result was legislation allowing a waiver of the aid cutoff to Pakistan until September 30, 1987, and a six year aid package of $3.2 billion (*CQ Almanac*, 1981, 181).

As Congressman Solarz summarized congressional sentiment on the issue,

There is more or less a consensus that, with 85,000 Soviet troops in Afghanistan and two million Afghan refugees in Pakistan, we have a real interest in providing economic and military assistance...Then the real question becomes, "What is the best way to go about it?" (*CQ Weekly Report*, December 5, 1981, 2414).

Members of Congress were torn between the obvious threat that Soviet expansionism into Afghanistan posed to American interests in the region, and the prospect of losing credibility by not punishing breaches of nuclear export agreements. Moreover, Congress wanted to be sure that it maintained a check on an executive whose commitment to nonproliferation was already suspect.

Part of the administration's proposal to resume economic and military aid to Pakistan included the sale of 40 F-16 fighter planes to Pakistan under the rationale that making Pakistan feel secure against outside military threats would help to lessen its drive to gain nuclear capabilities. Arguing that the Symington amendment had been ineffective on either point, Under Secretary of State for Security Assistance James Buckley testified before the House Foreign Affairs Subcommittee,

No one doubts that the Pakistani government has been working as rapidly as possible toward the capability of a nuclear option. No one doubts that the Symington amendment has done nothing to stop it. [Sale of the F-16s would] give Pakistan the ability to handle, with its own resources, incursions and limited cross-border threats from Soviet-backed Afghan forces, and to keep the Soviets from thinking they can coerce and subvert Pakistan with impunity. [Further, it would] demonstrate that a strong security relationship exists between the U.S. and Pakistan which the Soviet Union must take into account in its calculations (*CQ Weekly Report*, December 5, 1981, 2413).

While Congress, in the end, allowed the waiver of the Symington Amendment for Pakistan, they did add an amendment to the International Security and Development Cooperation Act of 1981 requiring the president to report to Congress annually on the extent and effectiveness of IAEA safeguards at Pakistan's nuclear facilities and the current state of Pakistani nuclear capabilities (Donnelly, 1981, 16).

By 1981 more than 40 nations had nuclear facilities, and about half of those were able to supply nuclear materials and technology to non-nuclear states (*CQ Weekly Report*, July 11, 1981, 1224). Congressional fears concerning the proliferation policy of the new Reagan Administration were fueled by a campaign comment Reagan made in January 1980, in which he declared, "I don't think it's any of our business" what other nations do in terms of developing nuclear capabilities (*CQ Weekly Report*, July 11, 1981, 1224). After some fast footwork by his staff, Reagan quickly announced a retraction of that statement and declared his administration's commitment to "do everything in our power to prevent" nuclear proliferation (*CQ Weekly Report*, July 11, 1981, 1224).

When the administration policy was finally enunciated, however, it appeared to coincide more with the views of nuclear industry advocates than those of congressional proponents of strong non-proliferation policy. Laying the foundations of the Reagan Administration's "reliable supplier" theme, Undersecretary of State for Security Assistance, Science and Technology James Buckley testified before the Senate Governmental Affairs Subcommittee,

> The United States must remain an active participant in the field of international nuclear cooperation, and we must be sensitive to the role of nuclear power in reducing dependence on imported oil. We simply cannot afford to penalize trustworthy and responsible nations of the world because of the nuclear adventurism of a few countries (*CQ Weekly Report*, July 11, 1981, 1224).

Part of the rationale being proposed here is that the U.S. should actively assist non-nuclear states in acquiring materials for non-military nuclear needs in order to reduce their efforts to acquire such materials covertly (and risk losing all track of who has what capability). The administration further proposed increasing supplies of conventional arms to non-nuclear states in order to dampen their desire to gain nuclear weapons.

Lingering mistrust between the branches on the issue of nonproliferation was merely fortified on October 11, 1981, when an administration proposal for the handling of nonproliferation policy was leaked to *The Washington Post*.

> The proposal called for the transfer of all nuclear export responsibilities from the independent Nuclear Regulatory Commission to the State Department, the repeal of current U.S. statutory sanctions against countries seeking nuclear weapons,...the weakening of legislative restrictions prohibiting U.S. nuclear cooperation with nations lacking full-scope IAEA safeguards...and favored "minimization of the need for congressional review of executive branch actions" (Rydell, 1990, 7; *The Washington Post*, October 11, 1981).

Despite the clear opposition to sales of nuclear materials to India in 1980 and 1981, the Reagan Administration again proposed to sell India nuclear technology in July 1982 during a visit by Prime Minister Indira

Gandhi. This time, however, it was proposed that the technology be received via France in order to skirt the restrictions in U.S. nonproliferation legislation. Not only did this violate the spirit of nonproliferation policy, but its success in getting around the letter of the laws was also questionable. The administration's determination to get the technology to India one way or another was clear, however, when Secretary of State George Shultz declared during a visit to India that if no other sources could be found the United States would supply India with its nuclear technology needs (*The New York Times*, October 2, 1983, A20).

A similar agreement was made with Argentina the same year to supply that Latin American country with a computer system for use in a plant intended to produce heavy water, critical to Argentina's nuclear fuel cycle. In addition, the administration approved the transfer of 143 tons of heavy water (originally produced in the United States) from West Germany to Argentina. Answering complaints that the administration had not consulted Congress before approving the transfer, Ambassador Richard Kennedy argued that the transfer was not covered under the law requiring congressional consultation (*The New York Times*, October 2, 1983, A20). Argentina, like India had refused to become a party to the 1969 U.N. Nonproliferation Treaty.

The Reagan Administration's determination to evade nonproliferation restrictions was becoming increasingly clear. Thus, when the Court ruled the legislative veto unconstitutional in June 1983 alarm spread among proponents of strong U.S. nonproliferation policy. Though they had not mustered the will among their colleagues to successfully curb administration transgressions of the spirit and letter of U.S. policy, now they had lost the one statutory mechanism which might give them the wherewithal to do so. As Senator Charles Percy (R-Ill.), Chairman of the Foreign Relations Committee lamented, "I am concerned that we as a nation--and in particular, we in Congress--may be losing our grip on nonproliferation." The *Chadha* decision, he feared would "profoundly change the effectiveness of the Nuclear Nonproliferation Act" (*The New York Times*, October 2, 1983, A20).

Those fears were realized in September 1983 when the Reagan Administration gave Westinghouse Corporation permission for the sale of replacement parts to South Africa for its Koeburg nuclear plant (*The New York Times*, October 2, 1983, A20). No longer did the administration feel the need to concern itself with using third parties to broker agreements for such materials.

The Reagan Administration's willingness to sacrifice nonproliferation policy to other foreign policy concerns was once again made clear in the proposal to sell China both high technology equipment and nuclear fuel in 1984. China, an acknowledged possessor of nuclear weapons was not only one of the few nuclear weapons states to refuse IAEA safeguards, but was also strongly believed to be supplying nuclear materials and technology to Pakistan, Argentina and Brazil. Under the 1978 Nuclear Non-Proliferation Act, China should have been barred from receiving any U.S. nuclear exports or aid. Though administration officials declared themselves satisfied with public and private assurances from the Chinese that China would not assist third countries in nuclear materials or technology, congressional members on both sides of the aisle remained skeptical.

Under the NNPA (1978) the agreement with China was subject to a joint (not concurrent) resolution from Congress within 90 days or else the agreement became binding. Unwilling to go so far as to pass a joint resolution of disapproval, which would kill the agreement altogether, Congress instead passed a joint resolution of *approval* which incorporated several restrictions before the actual transfer to China could take place. Specifically, the president was directed to certify to Congress that arrangements had been reached with China that any U.S. nuclear exports to that country were to be used solely for peaceful purposes (but did not go so far as to require full scope IAEA safeguards); that China provide additional information about its nonproliferation policies; required China to get permission from the United States before it could enrich U.S.-supplied uranium or reprocess spent U.S.-supplied reactor fuel; and barred nuclear licenses or transfers to China until the president sent Congress a report detailing the history of, and current developments in, China's nuclear nonproliferation policies (*CQ Almanac*, 1985, 112).

In the end, the resolution of approval was passed, though with lukewarm support. One observer noted that despite opposition from both liberals and conservatives, "the measure cleared because members realized the agreement would go into effect without any conditions if Congress failed to act" at all (*CQ Almanac*, 1985, 111). Edward Markey (D-Mass) lamented that at least the conditions on the resolution were "better than nothing" (*Cq Almanac*, 1985, 111). The agreement, providing nuclear fuel, equipment and technology to China was the first between the United States and a communist country.

Commenting on the implications of this episode for congressional-executive relations, Bruce Jentleson concluded, "By adding some conditions and restrictions but drawing the line at a damaging amendment, Congress managed to modify the policy without undoing the agreement. In doing so it showed that it had learned how to be nondeferential yet cooperative" (Jentleson, 1990, 194).

This may, however, be an overly optimistic assessment of the episode. In fact, the conditions added to the resolution were among the weakest of those proposed. Another amendment, stronger, and more true to the spirit of American nonproliferation policy was offered by Senator Glenn (D-Ohio) and would have required the equivalent of IAEA safeguards on China's nuclear programs. The amendment, attached to the 1986 appropriations resolution (HJ Res 465) was passed by the Senate and sent to the conference committee. After much squawking from the administration that the amendment would kill the agreement (despite the fact that China accepted similar conditions on nuclear imports from Japan) the conference committee agreed to kill the amendment (*CQ Almanac*, 1985, 112). The remaining conditions, although they require some additional paperwork and assurances from China, remain without teeth in the absence of any serious method of international inspection on China's use of U.S.-supplied materials. Rather than providing an example of effective interbranch codetermination of policy, as Jentleson suggests, the sale to China is more illustrative of nearly unilateral action by the administration, willing to accept minor (and ultimately evadable) conditions in order to ensure the success of its initiative.

Concerned about increasing loss of control over nonproliferation policy, and particularly the administration's preferences for short-term foreign policy gains over long-term nonproliferation goals, in August 1985, Congress passed an amendment to the Foreign Assistance Act of 1961 (Subsection 670[a][1][B]). It required a cutoff of aid to any country which attempts to illegally obtain materials or technology which would "contribute substantially" to its ability to build nuclear weapons. The cutoff, however, hinges on the president's determination that the materials and technology obtained are to be used in such a manner. In addition, this section required the president to certify whether Pakistan possessed a nuclear explosive, strengthening earlier provisions requiring merely that the president report on Pakistan's nuclear progress and the effectiveness of safeguards (Donnelly, 1990b, 1).

Congress was successful in cutting off all nuclear exports to South Africa as part of the Comprehensive Anti-Apartheid Act of 1986 (P.L.99-440), passed over presidential veto (Donnelly, 1990c, 5). Despite executive opposition, congressional action was fortified by strong public opinion against South Africa. This event marked one of the few instances in the past decade when public opinion has been galvanized enough to sustain congressional efforts to overcome executive opposition in a matter of foreign policy.

In 1987 the president was once again faced with certification of Pakistan's abstention from nuclear weapons development in order to continue aid to that country. The six year waiver granted in 1981 had ended, but the Soviet forces in Afghanistan remained. Just around the time of the certification debate, however, Arshad Pervez, a Pakistani national, was arrested and charged with conspiring to export nuclear materials to a retired Pakistani brigadier general. Three years earlier, 1984, three Pakistani nationals had been arrested in Houston attempting to smuggle parts for nuclear weapons out of the United States (*CQ Almanac*, 1987, 168). These incidents, in conjunction with intelligence reports of Pakistan's unabated attempts to gain greater nuclear capabilities inspired considerable skepticism about renewing aid.

Some of that skepticism was unveiled during hearings held by the Senate Committee on Governmental Affairs during February of 1987. Committee Chairman Glenn questioned Richard Kennedy, State Department Ambassador at Large:

> Glenn: Six years ago, at the strong urging of the administration, Congress provided over $3 billion in military and economic assistance to Pakistan and one of the key purposes of this assistance was to alleviate Pakistan's security concerns so that nuclear weapons would not be necessary. Is there any evidence you can provide the committee that Pakistan has given up its pursuit of a nuclear weapons capability?
> Kennedy: Senator, I think the record is clear publicly that we remained deeply concerned about Pakistan's nuclear program and its direction. It is also fair to say, however, that over those 6 years there has been restraint. There have been major efforts on our part to assure that that restraint occurs and we would like to see clearly a termination of any activities which might lead to the development of an explosive capability. We have made that absolutely clear to Pakistan (Hearings before the Committee on Governmental Affairs, February, 1987, 41).

Arguing that resumed aid to Pakistan would "reduce significantly the risk that Pakistan will possess a nuclear explosive device," (Reagan, 1987) and certifying that Pakistan did not already possess one, Reagan requested another six year waiver of aid restrictions and an aid package of $4 billion for Pakistan. Though opposed to the aid program, proponents of strong nonproliferation policy in Congress were unable to overcome the need to maintain Pakistan as a strong staging ground against Soviet occupation in Afghanistan. Though the Senate passed Reagan's request for the six year package, the House only approved the aid extension for two years (*CQ Almanac*, 1987, 168). The final legislation extended aid to Pakistan for two and a half years.

Once again in 1988, in spite of public recognition that Pakistan had in fact requested materials from the United States which were "to be used by Pakistan in the manufacture of a nuclear explosive device," Reagan determined that a waiver of the aid cutoff was "in the national interests of the United States" (Reagan, January 18, 1988; see also Rydell, 1990, 8). Pakistan was once again secure with American aid until April 1991.

Tensions between the administration and Congress over the issue of nonproliferation continue to percolate at times bubbling into the public spotlight. In August 1990, for example, Congressman John Dingell (D-Mich., Chairman, House Subcommittee on Oversight and Investigation), exasperated by the Department of Energy's refusal to supply information on Iraq's weapons capabilities and safeguards, obtained a court order to subpoena the information. In typical administration pseudo-cooperative style, DOE spokesman Tom Olsen replied, "The position of the Department of Energy is that we will give them anything, provided we have their request in writing, but, so far, they haven't done that. We will just consider the subpoena their written request" (*The Los Angeles Times*, August 21, 1990, A20).

Despite its inability to certify that Pakistan does not have a bomb, the Bush Administration has recently asked Congress to continue aid to that country (*Congressional Quarterly Weekly Report*, October 6, 1990, 3238). Congressional opposition to a waiver of the cutoff appeared strong. But concern over the war in the Persian Gulf overshadowed congressional consideration of Pakistan's aid renewal when it expired in April 1991. Advocates of strong nonproliferation policy have been fairly successful in rallying congressional sentiment against aid renewal in this most controversial of cases, particularly given the withdrawal of Soviet forces from Afghanistan and virtual disintegration of its military threat to the region. What's more, concern over Iraq's nuclear capabilities has raised public awareness of the potential dangers of proliferation all over the world, adding strength to the nonproliferation arguments.

If congressional sentiment does galvanize on the issue of Pakistan it will have to overcome both the problem of member commitment and the lack of a strong statutory device to impose its will. This is particularly true, given the past decade of nonproliferation policy when "despite congressional attempts to legislate policy, the executive branch has tended to follow its own agenda" (Clark, 1986, 900).

If indeed the Congress were to garner enough support to cut off aid to Pakistan it would need to be through an appropriations battle, likely to be high profile in nature. While a disapproval threat may compel executive consultation and compromise prior to arranging an aid package with Pakistan, history provides little evidence to sustain such an expectation.[10]

## Nonproliferation Policy and the Impact of *Chadha*

Nuclear nonproliferation policy presents a case in which there is an institutional motivation for Congress to get involved but less (or variable) individual motivation. For this reason, congressional will to stand up to the executive is only intermittent, catalyzed mainly by either an egregious flaunting of American export requirements by a third country or by public pressure. In those instances when Congress does take an active stance, it is usually in response to executive neglect or coincides with the executive policy position. In cases of policy disagreement, Congress is reluctant to put up decisive opposition.

During the Nixon and Ford Administrations, the relatively lax interest in the issue led to substantial legislative initiative but not necessarily a high degree of conflict. Under Carter there was an interesting contrast between the early and later periods of his administration. In the early part (1976-1978) executive and congressional policy stances were coincident, making for a cooperative relationship between the branches. In later years (1979-1980) disputes over aid to Pakistan and the sale of fuel to India split congressional and executive opinion. Carter's strong interest in the issue of nonproliferation from the start, and congressional fears that he was now abandoning that stance, led both sides to feel that they were the standardbearer of nonproliferation policy for the United States. In the case of the sale of nuclear fuel to India, therefore, Congress did use the threat of the legislative veto to try to back down the president, but ultimately lacked the will (particularly in the Senate) to kill the sale. Whether this was because there was no strong domestic constituency pushing against the sale, or because the president was able to cast the issue as one of geostrategic and national security importance (Baker, 1984, 154) remains under debate.

During the Reagan Administration, executive policy was so clearly hostile to legislative intent in the NNPA and the Glenn-Symington amendments, that Congress once again felt the need to become actively involved in redirecting the executive course of nonproliferation policy. Under Reagan, like Carter, executive propriety was fairly high on this issue with many in the administration taking a strong stance in favor of creating a "new realism" in American nuclear export policy. But in spite of policy disagreement and congressional dissatisfaction, the motivation of members to stand up to the executive on this issue was flagging.

The *Chadha* decision, therefore, did affect the ability of Congress to impact U.S. nuclear nonproliferation policy, but the impact was dulled by the fact that congressional will to use the statutory tool was weak.

Because the majority of legislators lack strong motivation to assert themselves on the issue, the loss of the legislative veto was probably more a symbolic blow to Congress than a substantive one. The nature of the nonproliferation issue, like other strategic-nonsalient issues, is such that Congress is unlikely to "go to the mat" against the president with any regularity.

Policy disagreement between the executive and legislative branches is a necessary yet not sufficient condition for conflict. In the case of nuclear nonproliferation, the other criteria (particularly electoral motivation and congressional will to act) are not satisfied. Thus conflict is only moderately likely, and intermittent in nature, and the loss of the legislative veto has been a secondary issue.

# 8

---

# Crisis Policy, the Executive Domain:
# The War Powers Resolution

The final case study illustrates an issue type in which the loss of the legislative veto has had no practical impact on congressional-executive relations in foreign policy making.[11] Crisis issues are those in which American territory, citizens or interests are threatened. They require quick and decisive action, and represent the type of twentieth century foreign policy demands which the eighteenth century institutional structure is least equipped to handle. Indeed, it is in crisis situations that one would expect the legislative veto to be an ideal accommodation to the dual needs of executive flexibility in action and congressional oversight. In practice, however, since World War II most presidents have claimed inherent executive powers for unilateral action in crises, while Congress has generally been relieved to dole away responsibility. As a consequence, the use of the legislative veto has been moot in practice, if not in theory.

The case of the War Powers Resolution classically illustrates congressional-executive relations in the process of crisis foreign policy. The resolution was the legislative manifestation of congressional reassertion against an executive who had broken free of oversight and control. And yet, ironically, it is also representative of the type of issue in which legislators are least inclined to take over the reins of policy making.

Of the many tools and devices available to a government to conduct its foreign policy, the power to threaten or engage in war is by far the most potent. It is also the most controversial.

The divisions and uncertainties over who should hold the power to commit the nation to armed conflict is reflected both in the arguments of the Founding Fathers and in the Constitution which they produced. One often noted example was the last minute, and successful, efforts by James Madison and Elbridge Gerry during the Constitutional Convention to change the wording of the powers delegated to Congress from the power to "make" war to the power to "declare" war (Madison, 1987). This distinction was precisely designed to afford the executive the flexibility to react to emergency situations without having to gain the consent of the deliberative and often inertia-plagued legislature.

Still, there was an acute awareness of the dangers of giving the president too much leeway in such a critical area. Even the great defender of executive powers, Alexander Hamilton, warned against committing the "interests of so delicate and momentous a kind, as those which concern its intercourse with the rest of the world, to the sole disposal of a magistrate created and circumstanced as would be a President of the United States" (Hamilton, Federalist No. 75, 451).

Though he recognized the president as commander-in-chief, he gave such status considerably less power than is generally presumed today, arguing,

> It would amount to nothing more than the supreme command and direction of the military and naval forces, as first general and admiral of the Confederacy; while that of the British king extends to the *declaring* of war and to the *raising* and *regulating* of fleets and armies--all which, by the Constitution under consideration, would appertain to the legislature (emphasis original) (Federalist No. 69, 418).

Since President Washington declared United States neutrality in the war between England and France debate has raged over the proper balance of power between the executive and legislature. Even during the period following World War II, a time generally noted for its unusual degree of consensus over the broad goals of foreign policy in the United States, the debate over the distribution of power between the executive and legislative branches never ceased. Frustration within Congress over the "imperial presidents'" (Schlesinger, 1973) clear dominance in the realm of foreign affairs led to what appeared to be a strong congressional reassertion with the passage of the War Powers Resolution in 1973. For the first time in the post-war era Congress appeared to enact legislation which carried the real potential of reestablishing that body as a serious participant in the decisions of this country to use its most potent weapon: its military power.

President Nixon vetoed the War Powers Resolution, calling it "unconstitutional and dangerous to the best interests of our Nation" (Crabb and Holt, 1989, 143; Henkin, 1990, 30). The override of Nixon's veto by a vote of 284-135 in the House and 75-18 in the Senate appeared to demonstrate Congress' new-found resolve (Warburg, 1989, 126). As subsequent events have revealed, however, that resolve has been shown to be little more than temporary breastbeating. By most accounts the War Powers Resolution has proven a failure.

## Determining the Potential for Conflict

Examining the issue in the theoretical framework presented in this work illustrates why that has been the case and why it should come as little surprise. The passage of legislation, even as seemingly powerful as the War Powers Resolution, could not remedy the underlying reasons that Congress has failed as a codeterminor of American commitments to military action abroad.

### Institutional Motives for Congressional Action

Institutionally, it is clear that Congress has a strong motivation to participate in the decision making process concerning the use of military power. The Constitution, though it overlaps the powers of the legislature and the executive in this area, clearly gives Congress responsibility for raising and supporting the armed forces and, of course, declaring war (Article 1, Section 8). Many argue in addition that the power to issue letters of marque and reprisal show the Founders' clear intent to have Congress take the lead in international interaction since at the time the Constitution was written such letters were the basis for peaceful or warlike relations (Schlesinger, 1988, 1230; Deering, 1989). In Schlesinger's view, "The Framers, in short, envisaged a partnership between Congress and the president in the conduct of foreign affairs with Congress as the senior partner" (Schlesinger, 1988, 1231).

In the congressional resurgence of the 1970s many point to the War Powers Resolution (1973) as the watershed act in foreign policy. The legislation was designed to reclaim Congress' institutional role in determining American military involvements. Though Congress itself was partly to blame for the shifting of foreign policy authority to the president, legislators' disillusionment with imperious presidents reawakened a sense of institutional responsibility and power.

But this reawakened spirit did not eliminate the political disincentives for congressional assertion in crisis foreign policy. Thus, while institutional motivation is high, the costs of opposing presidents in crisis situations renders electoral motivation low, and congressional assertion limited to rhetoric.


### Electoral Motives for Congressional Action

Legislators' electoral motivation to oppose the president in war powers is undermined by the negative public perception of representatives challenging the American leader at a time when the nation should stand in solid support behind him. The issue of war powers arises, of course, only at times of crisis or potential crisis involving American troops, citizens or national interests. It is thus unique because the time frame for consideration of action is severely limited. Presidents have been very successful in portraying such times as necessitating decisive action based upon information which only the president has full access to. These are the times when the country "rallies 'round the flag."

To even imply dissension within the ranks has generally been a risky proposition for members of Congress who see a clear opportunity to fall into line with the majority of their constituents by backing the president. As Whalen has noted, "(t)here appears to be a direct correlation between public opinion polls and Congress' willingness to question presidential military expeditions" (Whalen, 1982, 64). Though the vote in Congress concerning the authorization of force against Iraq following its invasion of Kuwait may show an increased tolerance for congressional reservation in times of crisis, historically this has not been the case. It should also be noted, however, that the marginal vote favoring authorization of force reflected a corresponding split in public opinion.

As policy entrepreneurs, war powers offers a potential forum from which to establish credentials in foreign policy. This is especially attractive to senators with presidential aspirations. But caution must be taken, since a vocal stance against the president (often perceived as against national solidarity) can become a serious liability at reelection time.

The balance of institutional and electoral motivations in war powers, then, leads to the expectation that Congress will become involved in the issue but that involvement will be strongly moderated by the president's (and general public's) position. When Congress does become involved, however, the encounters are likely to inspire conflict over the *process* of decision making if not the actual *substance* of policy. Specifically, Congress is likely to defend its institutional prerogatives as partner in the decision making process even as it acquiesces to executive policy. What conflict does ensue, therefore, stems from Congress' attempts to make itself heard institutionally while it lacks the will to statutorily enforce its demands. This is compounded by an extraordinary degree of executive propriety in the area of war powers.

## Congressional Will to Act

Both supporters of congressional reassertion in foreign policy and opponents agree that the critical flaw in the War Powers Resolution has been Congress' lack of will in enforcing its provisions. In passing the original legislation a compromise was worked out in conference which dropped from the Senate version the specific criteria under which the president would be obliged to report military action to Congress per Subsection 4(a)(1), the provision which automatically triggers a time limit on troop deployment (Javits, 1987). The resulting legislation leaves it primarily to executive discretion to determine whether the involvement of American military personnel should be reported under the provision or under one of the other provisions which would not trigger the clock. (The exact provisions of the resolution are discussed in detail below). Though Congress does have the power itself to determine that the military action qualifies under section 4(a)(1), and thus begin the time limitations, it has only once had the will to enforce this prerogative. Yet even in this instance the congressional action was only taken as part of a compromise worked out with the president to extend the authority for troop deployment for 18 months (the Multinational Forces in Lebanon Resolution). As will become clear through the history of noncompliance discussed below, the combination of executive flaunting of the War Powers Resolution requirements along with the lack of congressional will to enforce its provisions has undermined both the threat of the War Powers Resolution and its effectiveness in practice. This has only fortified the claims of successive presidents that war powers fall under the domain of executive powers and the commander-in-chief provision of the Constitution.

According to historian and former government official Arthur Schlesinger, the extreme executive sense of control over American military power comes from "an extravagant interpretation of the commander-in-chief clause.." and "a misreading of the Court's 1936 decision in the *Curtiss-Wright* case." Though some interpret the decision in *Curtiss-Wright* to "vindicate the idea of inherent and unilateral presidential power to go to war," Schlesinger argues that in fact the case did not even involve the war-making power. (It) involved, not the question of the president's right to act without congressional authority, but the question of his right to act under and in accord with an act of Congress. Yet the present administration somehow manages to champion a theory of inherent presidential prerogative in foreign affairs that would have appalled the Founding Fathers (Schlesinger, 1988, 1232; see also Henkin, 1990).

The president's dominant position in policy making during crisis situations, such as those which evoke debate over war powers, is further enhanced by the international context pitting American interests against those of a foreign country's. Under such circumstances, substantive policy considerations are often overshadowed by nationalistic rhetoric. Again, it's the rally-'round-the-flag effect. Debate over the long-term policy implications of short-term action is often relegated to the sidelines.

## Conflict Between the Branches

Subsection 5(c) provides that in the event United States Armed Forces are engaged in hostilities without a declaration of war or specific congressional authorization, Congress may order their withdrawal by concurrent resolution (legislative veto). In spite of the potential for conflict between the branches on the issue, the *Chadha* decision has had little if any impact on the actual effectiveness of the War Powers Resolution. In essence, the legislative veto provision never really constituted the "teeth" of the resolution, the mechanism which would compel executive compliance. The real threat from the Congress came in subsection 4(a)(1) which would trigger the timetable for mandatory withdrawal. The legislative veto, therefore, was somewhat redundant.

More importantly, however, the *Chadha* decision has not substantively affected Congress' leverage over war powers because even before the Court's decision Congress never had the will to credibly threaten to use the legislative veto . Given the reasons stated above, if Congress did not have the fortitude to compel the president to report under the provisions of subsection 4(a)(1)-- which would at least give the administration time to try to persuade Congress to extend authorization for the operation-- it was very unlikely to enact a legislative veto which would abruptly undercut both the president and the troops in the field.

Because of the politics surrounding the issue of war powers, it has been clear that regardless of the statutory tools available, Congress is unwilling to seriously challenge executive policy. In short, without the will to use it, the inclusion of the legislative veto in the War Powers Resolution has been moot since the day of its enactment.

Figure 8.1 presents the number of bills and resolutions introduced in opposition to the president over war powers as a percentage of all bills and resolutions introduced in the 95th to 101st Congresses. As the data demonstrate, the level of conflict between the branches has not been significantly affected by the loss of the legislative veto. Though there have been a number of bills introduced in the wake of *Chadha*, a closer examination reveals that most of these attempt to fortify the original War Powers Resolution but do not necessarily refer to the legislative veto provision. These efforts come in fits and starts, however, and no sustained pattern of increased conflict emerges.

Though there has been debate over whether the *Chadha* decision[12] negates the entire War Powers Resolution, it is reasonably clear from

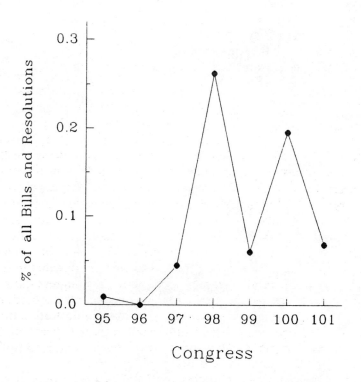

FIGURE 8.1  Bills and Resolutions: War Powers (95th-101st Congress).

recent court interpretations that the separability clause in Section 9 leaves the remainder of the resolution intact. (A decisive verdict is unlikely, however, as courts have repeatedly been unwilling to decide cases involving war powers.) To be certain, Congress substituted the concurrent resolution provision for a joint resolution in the 1983 State Department Authorization Bill (S 1324) (Collier, 1988, 11).

Congress' real goal has been to be a visible participant in policy making rather than the primary (or even co-equal) designer of policy. The debates surrounding war powers have thus been based upon institutional facesaving rather than substantive policy choices. Of course, during the height of protest over the Vietnam War Congress was compelled by constituency pressure to press for substantive policy change. Even then, however, it settled for sense-of-the-Congress resolutions which had no legally binding authority. In spite of rhetoric to the contrary, Congress is, and has been, content to leave responsibility for American military action squarely in the lap of the president. What it wants is to participate in the policy making process yet evade accountability for the policy making outcome. It is hardly surprising, therefore, that the loss of the legislative veto has had no substantive effect on congressional-executive relations in this area of foreign policy.

In spite of recent efforts to "put teeth" into the War Powers Resolution, the underlying problem remains congressional will. Unless legislators can somehow change the circumstances which mitigate against serious congressional involvement in restricting executive flexibility in the use of American military force, no statutory windowdressing can provide a substitute.

## Provisions of the War Powers Resolution

The War Powers Resolution contained statutory mechanisms potentially capable of compelling executive consultation. Those mechanisms are discussed in this section. The substantive value (as opposed to potential value) of those mechanisms has been debatable. In the end, the impact which the War Powers Resolution holds rests upon congressional will to enforce its provisions. Congressional will in this regard has been meager.

While the legislative veto was included in the War Powers Resolution, and has been a source of considerable controversy, the provision which really gives the resolution its teeth is the mandatory withdrawal requirement in Section 4(a)(1). A brief discussion of the statute's provisions will help to illuminate the reasons that the resolution has been so controversial, and why it has been largely ineffectual as a tool of congressional leverage.

Sections 3 and 4 of the resolution concern the reporting and consultation requirements. Section 3 states that

> The President *in every possible instance* shall consult with Congress before introducing United States Armed Forces into hostilities or into situations where imminent involvement in hostilities is clearly indicated by the circumstances, and after every such introduction shall consult regularly with the Congress until United States Armed Forces are no longer engaged in hostilities or have been removed from such situations (emphasis added) (P.L. 93-148).

Section 4(a) lays out the conditions under which the president is required to report to Congress. They are:

> in the absence of a declaration of war, in any case in which United States Armed Forces are introduced--
> 1) into hostilities or into situations where imminent involvement in hostilities is clearly indicated by the circumstances;
> 2) into the territory, airspace or waters of a foreign nation, while equipped for combat...[supply and training missions exempted];
> 3) in numbers which substantially enlarge United States Armed Forces equipped for combat already located in a foreign nation; the President shall submit within 48 hours to the Speaker of the House of Representatives and to the President pro tempore of the Senate a report, in writing setting forth--
> A) the circumstances necessitating the introduction of United States Armed Forces;
> B) the constitutional and legislative authority under which such introduction took place; and
> C) the estimated scope and duration of the hostilities or involvement. (PL 93-148).

Subsections 4(b) and (c) stipulate that the president shall provide the Congress with any other information which it requests concerning the military action, and that concerning reports on the status of the operation "in no event shall he report to the Congress less often than once every six months."

Subsection 4(a)(1) is the most sensitive element of the resolution since reports made under this provision trigger subsection 5(b) which stipulates that

> Within sixty calendar days after a report is submitted or is required to be submitted pursuant to section 4(a)(1), whichever is earlier, the

President shall terminate any use of United States Armed Forces with respect to which such report was submitted (or required to be submitted), unless the Congress (1) has declared war or has enacted a specific authorization for such use of the United States Armed Forces, (2) has extended by law such sixty-day period, or (3) is physically unable to meet as a result of an armed attack upon the United States.

The 60 day limitation may be extended by another 30 days if the president "determines and certifies to Congress in writing" that such an extension is necessary for the safe withdrawal of the troops.

Subsection 5(a) provides the steps for congressional consideration of the report, while 5(c) is the legislative veto mechanism. It states,

Notwithstanding subsection (b), at any time that United States Armed Forces are engaged in hostilities outside the territory of the United States, its possessions and territories without a declaration of war or specific statutory authorization, such forces shall be removed by the President if Congress so directs by concurrent resolution.

Section 6 stipulates the congressional priority procedures for considering reports and legislation under the War Powers Resolution. Section 7 lays out the priority procedures for concurrent resolutions under subsection 5(c), and Section 8 discusses what the War Powers Resolution should (and should not) be interpreted to mean.

Section 9 is an important inclusion in light of court rulings concerning legislative vetoes. It is the "separability clause" stating that "If any provision of this joint resolution or the application thereof to any person or circumstance is held invalid, the remainder of the joint resolution and the application of such provision to any other person or circumstance shall not be affected thereby."

This section makes clear the legislative intent at the time the War Powers Resolution was written. The power of the resolution was not meant to rest primarily upon the concurrent resolution, nor any other single provision, contained within. In the wake of the *Chadha* decision, courts have used the separability criterion as critical in the determination of whether various statutes containing legislative vetoes should be declared unconstitutional in their entirety.

Section 10, the final section of the War Powers Resolution, merely states that the resolution shall take effect on the date of its enactment (PL 93-148).

Thus while the legislative veto included in the War Powers Resolution is clearly there to increase potential congressional leverage vis-a-vis the executive, it has not been considered the most menacing element of the resolution. Had Congress ever used the veto, or for that matter even seriously threatened to use it, views on subsection 5(c) may be considerably different. As it stands, however, Congress has primarily emphasized the reporting requirement of subsection 4(a)(1) which would trigger the withdrawal of troops under 5(b). This is not particularly surprising, since in times of conflict or potential conflict Congress is reluctant to undermine the flexibility of the president. Subsection 5(b) gives Congress a significant role to play in the decision to engage U.S. troops in conflict without assuming the primary responsibility for the development of such a policy.

Since the enactment of the War Powers Resolution, presidents have argued that the provision in 5(b) is unconstitutional because it allows Congress to compel withdrawal of troops through inaction. Recall that *unless* Congress takes positive action to extend the stay of deployments or declares war the troops must be withdrawn. Not only does this hamstring the president's ability to conduct foreign policy, critics argue, but it entirely evades the legislative process. A final settlement of this argument appears unlikely, however, as repeated attempts (usually by Congressmen) to test the constitutionality of the War Powers Resolution have been turned back by the courts. Citing the "political questions doctrine" a number of courts have declared the issue "nonjusticiable" -- it must be resolved by political settlement. The court merely reiterates the Constitution's "invitation to struggle" (Corwin, 1957).

Much of congressional "assertion" in war powers has depended upon the cooperation of the president for its effect. The apparent gains made during the Eisenhower Administration were largely the result of the president's views on the necessity of congressional cooperation rather than legislative initiatives. Similarly, the one time that Congress unilaterally declared a troop deployment subject to section 4(a)(1), and hence time limitation (the Multinational Forces in Lebanon Resolution), it was the result of an agreement with the president to extend authorization for an additional 18 months. Yet Congress did not need to wait until the president agreed to report military actions under subsection 4(a)(1) in order to enforce the time limits of the War Powers Resolution. Like Dorothy and her ruby slippers, Congress had the power all along.

There were two ways in which Congress could invoke the time limits in subsection 5(b). First, Congress could pass independent legislation stipulating that the military action undertaken does fall under the criterion of "imminent hostilities" stipulated in subsection 4(a)(1) and thus triggers subsection 5(b). This was the purpose of the Multinational Forces in Lebanon Resolution.

The second way is, ironically through inaction. In a recent work examining the constitutional aspects of War Powers Resolution, Glennon has argued:

> The notion of "invoking" the Resolution also wrongly implies presidential discretion in submission of reports. In fact, the wording of section 4(a)(1) is clear, and no discretion exists; if events occur that constitute "hostilities or...situations where imminent involvement in hostilities is clearly indicated by the circumstances," a report must be submitted. That the sixty-day period commences when a report is "required to be submitted" reinforces this conclusion. This provision makes it clear that presidential noncompliance with the reporting requirement of section 4(a)(1) will not defeat the operation of the Resolution; the running of the period will still be triggered if the specified events occur....It would have made no sense for Congress to require that if the President violates the law by failing to report, the onus would then be on Congress to pass a law "invoking" (presumably triggering) the time period....The argument underscores the apparently undisputed legislative intent that no congressional action would be required to trigger the running of the period (Glennon, 1990, 91-92).

According to Glennon's argument, presumably, even the first option of passing legislation is unnecessary, and all Congress needs to do is to proceed with deliberation under the provisions of the War Powers Resolution as to the granting or denying of authority to continue the military action. While invoking the time limitations could therefore be achieved through inaction, its consequence would be to require positive action (approval or disapproval of the military deployment) on the part of Congress. This would, of course, put the ball in Congress' court and bring with it both accountability and responsibility for policy--neither of which Congress wants. We are back to square one. Despite the potential value of the statutory mechanisms, without congressional will to enforce them they are meaningless.

The other provision potentially giving Congress the power to override executive use of U.S. military force is the legislative veto provision in 5(c), or in the post-*Chadha* era the joint resolution of disapproval. In some ways this is an even more direct lever for congressional action since it can be undertaken regardless of the way that the military action is reported and without specific time allowances. Yet these mechanisms too would place Congress in the position of responsibility both for policy and for publicly reversing the decision of the executive. In the case of the joint resolution of disapproval it is practically inconceivable that Congress would both disapprove a policy and override the inevitable veto to follow. At the same time they would risk a high profile confrontation, creating the appearance of an obstructive legislature undermining national unity and prestige in the face of an international crisis. Even institutional facesaving is insufficient to overcome the damage which such an image would do to the individual, reelection-minded, members of Congress.

Many argue, correctly, that one of the main problems of the War Powers Resolution is its failure to address specifically the two most common types of conflict which nations face in the late 20th century: covert operations and short-term military strikes (Koh, 1990, 39; Crabb and Holt, 1989; Ambrose, 1988). This failure can only be attributed to a lack of rigor on the part of Congress, given the long history of such techniques dating well before the Vietnam War. The defense of the War Powers Resolution often revolves around the determination of its authors to neither undercut nor widen the powers delegated to the legislative and executive branches in the Constitution, rather to empower them in a contemporary form. This explanation pales, however, when one considers that even at the writing of the Constitution the Founders were well aware that "the ceremony of a formal denunciation of war has of late fallen into disuse (Hamilton, Federalist No. 25, 165; Deering, 1989, 4).

Yet even in the provisions of the resolution which implicitly acknowledge the grey areas of military conflict short of war, the wording is often so vague as to constitute an enormous loophole. In Section 3, for example, the president is required to consult with Congress "in every possible instance" before committing troops. Presidents have repeatedly argued that the circumstances surrounding a given incident required such swift action as to preclude consultation with Congress beforehand. In the best of circumstances the executive has consulted with Congress *before* action actually takes place, but well after the decision to take action had been made. Unless Congress is willing to abort military actions there is little it can do to compel consultation "in every possible instance." In addition, the nature of contemporary conflict is such that by the time Congress can gear up to deliberate on the lack of consultation, the military action is already over--take for example the ill-fated rescue attempt of the hostages in Iran, or the invasion of Grenada.

Similarly, 4(a)(1) requires reports to be submitted "when imminent involvement in hostilities is clearly indicated." Clearly to whom? Again, presidents have successfully argued that the circumstances surrounding troop deployment have not clearly indicated imminent hostilities--even in such implausible situations as Lebanon and the Persian Gulf. In a number of cases troops have even received danger pay, yet apparently do not face "imminent hostilities." Again, had it the will, Congress could declare military actions subject to 4(a)(1). As it stands, the legislature has been willing to leave such determinations to the president, widening the loophole and allowing ridiculous categorizations of military actions.

Looking at the legislative history of the War Powers Resolution shows that even when attempting to clarify its intent Congress has left the provisions extremely murky. For example, subsection 4(a)(3) requires reports to Congress when a troop deployment occurs "in numbers which substantially enlarge U.S. Armed Forces" in a given area. The House Report explaining this provision reads:

> While the word "substantially" designates a flexible criterion, it is possible to arrive at a common-sense understanding of the numbers involved. A 100% increase in numbers of Marine guards at an embassy--say from 5 to 10--clearly would not be an occasion for a report. A thousand additional men sent to Europe under present circumstances does not significantly enlarge the total U.S. troop strength of about 300,000 already there. However, the dispatch of 1,000 men to Guantanamo Bay, Cuba, which now has a complement of 4,000 would mean an increase of 25%, which is substantial. Under this circumstance, President Kennedy would have been required to report to Congress in 1962 when he raised the number of U.S. military advisers in Vietnam from 700 to 16,000 (U.S. Congress House Report 93-287, 7; see also Collier, 1988, 14).

While this explanation lays out some "common sense" parameters, it does little to clarify the requirement in the vast majority of potential cases, again leaving a gaping loophole for executive discretion.

The original Senate version of the War Powers Resolution would have gone some of the distance in spelling out the president's powers as commander-in-chief: "to defend our nation in its states and possessions; to defend our Armed Forces wherever they were; to implement the directions of Congress as to initiating war; and to protect, defend and rescue U.S. citizens in danger wherever they might be" (Javits, 1987, 57). Yet true to form, these provisions are also sufficiently vague as to impose little restraint upon the president. As with the final version of the War Powers Resolution, lacking the will to enforce its intentions, it makes little difference how clearly the requirements are stated.

### The War Powers Resolution: A History of Noncompliance

In United States history Congress has declared war only four times: the War of 1812; the Spanish-American War; World War I; and World War II. In a fifth instance, the Mexican-American War, Congress passed a joint resolution authorizing engagement (Katzmann, 1990, 450). Yet the U.S. military has been involved in over 200 "actions"--some of which have been commonly referred to as wars (Korea, Vietnam, the Persian Gulf). Limiting the ability of presidents to involve U.S. forces in precipitous actions without congressional consent was the primary purpose for the enactment of the War Powers Resolution.

Since its enactment in 1973 presidents have reported to the Congress twenty-three times on matters which would fall under the guidelines of the War Powers Resolution. In a number of other instances, at least ten of particular note, which may arguably have fallen under the resolution's domain, no reports have been submitted (Collier, 1990). In only one instance, the Mayaguez incident, was the report submitted under subsection 4(a)(1) of the War Powers Resolution. Presidents since Nixon have submitted reports "taking note of" or "consistent with" the resolution, but never "in compliance with" or "pursuant to" its requirements. Presidents have never acknowledged the validity of the resolution, a tradition carried on in full force by President Bush.

Table 8.1 lists the formal reports made to Congress in conjunction with the War Powers Resolution.

TABLE 8.1 Formal Reports Made to Congress Concerning War Powers

| | | |
|---|---|---|
| April 4, 1975 | Danang | Citing subsection 4(a)(2) President Ford reported the use of Navy and Marines to evacuate refugees from Danang and other seaports in Vietnam. |
| April 12, 1975 | Cambodia | Taking note of sections 4 and 4(a)(2) President Ford reported the use of Marines to evacuate U.S. personnel from Cambodia. |
| April 30, 1979 | Vietnam | Taking note of section 4 President Ford reported the use of Marines to evacuate U.S. personnel from South Vietnam. |
| May 15, 1975 | Mayaguez | Taking note of section 4(a)(1) President Ford reported (after- the-fact) that U.S. military had been used to retake the ship Mayaguez, seized by the Cambodian Navy. |

144

Table 8.1 (continued)

| April 26, 1980 | Iran | Consistent with the WPR President Carter reported (after-the-fact) the use of U.S. military helicopters in an unsuccessful attempt to rescue U.S. hostages held in the embassy in Iran. |
|---|---|---|
| March 19, 1982 | Sinai | Consistent with subsection 4(a)(2) President Reagan reported the deployment of U.S. troops to the Multinational Force and Observers (MFO) to assist in enforcing the 1981 Egypt-Israeli peace treaty. |
| August 24, 1982 | Lebanon | Consistent with the WPR President Reagan reported the use of 800 Marines as part of a multinational force overseeing the withdrawal of PLO members from Lebanon. |
| Sept. 29, 1982 | Lebanon | Consistent with the WPR President Reagan reported the participation of 1200 Marines in the multinational force to restore the sovereignty of the Lebanese government. |
| August 8, 1983 | Chad | Consistent with Section 4 President Reagan reported sending two AWACS and eight F-15 fighters to Sudan to help the Chadian government fight Libyan-supported rebels. |
| August 30, 1983 | Lebanon | Consistent with Section 4 President Reagan submitted a report after Marines serving in the multinational force were fired upon, killing two. |
| October 25, 1983 | Grenada | Consistent with the WPR President Reagan reported that Army and Marine troops had begun landing on the island of Grenada to restore law and order and evacuate U.S. medical students. |
| March 26, 1986 | Libya | Without mentioning the WPR President Reagan reported (after-the-fact) that U.S. forces had fired missiles at Libyan vessels and the Libyan missile site Sitre in response to a Libyan attack during freedom of navigation exercises. |

Table 8.1 (continued)

| April 16, 1986 | Libya | Consistent with the WPR President Reagan reported (after-the-fact) that U.S. air and naval forces had bombed terrorist facilities and military installations in Libya. |
|---|---|---|
| Sept. 23, 1987 | Persian Gulf | In the "spirit of mutual cooperation" (but not in compliance with the WPR) President Reagan reported (after-the-fact) that two U.S. helicopters had fired on Iranian vessels observed laying mines in the Gulf. |
| October 10, 1987 | Persian Gulf | Consistent with the WPR President Reagan reported (after-the-fact) that three U.S. helicopters, returning fire from Iranian naval vessels, sank one of the boats. |
| October 20, 1987 | Persian Gulf | Consistent with the WPR President Reagan reported (after-the-fact) the U.S. destruction of an Iranian armed platform used for attack and mine laying purposes in retaliation for an Iranian silkworm missile attack against the U.S.-flagged tanker *Sea Isle City*. |
| April 19, 1988 | Persian Gulf | Consistent with the WPR President Reagan reported (after-the-fact) that U.S. forces had "neutralized" an Iranian oil platform after the U.S.S. Samuel B. Roberts hit a mine and other Iranian attacks. |
| July 4, 1988 | Persian Gulf | Consistent with the WPR President Reagan reported (after-the-fact) that two U.S. Naval ships had sunk two Iranian vessels. In addition, one of the ships, the U.S.S. Vincennes had shot down an Iranian civilian airliner thinking it to be a hostile military aircraft. |
| July 14, 1988 | Persian Gulf | Consistent with the WPR President Reagan reported (after-the-fact) that two U.S. helicopters exchanged fire with two small Iranian boats while responding to a distress call from a Japanese-owned Panamanian tanker. |

Table 8.1 (continued)

| Dec. 2, 1989 | Philippines | Consistent with the WPR President Bush reported that U.S. planes had taken off from Clark Air Base to provide air cover to the government of Corazon Aquino during a coup attempt, to restore order, and to protect Americans in the Philippines. |
| Dec. 21, 1989 | Panama | Consistent with the WPR President Bush reported that he had decided to order U.S. military forces into Panama to protect the 35,000 American citizens there, restore the democratic process, preserve the integrity of the Panama Canal treaties, and apprehend General Manuel Noriega. |
| August 6, 1990 | Liberia | Though not citing the WPR, President Bush reported (after-the-fact) that that Marines had been sent to Liberia to protect the American embassy in Monrovia and evacuate American citizens. |
| August 9, 1990 | Saudi Arabia | Consistent with the WPR President Bush (after-the-fact) reported that he had ordered two squadrons of F-15s and one brigade of the 82nd Airborne Division into Saudi Arabia to keep Iraqi leader Saddam Hussein from invading Saudi Arabia. Kuwait had already been invaded by Hussein on August 2. |

Source: Adapted from Collier, 1988, 1990.

Those events which were not formally reported to Congress, many of which have been a source of controversy between the branches are reported in Table 8.2.

TABLE 8.2 Events Not Formally Reported to Congress Concerning War Powers

| | | |
|---|---|---|
| July 22-23, 1974 | Cyprus | U.S. Navy helicopters were used to evacuate approximately 500 Americans and foreign nationals from Cyprus. |
| June 20, 1976 | Lebanon | U.S. Navy landing craft were used to evacuate 263 Americans and Europeans from Lebanon during factional fighting. |
| August 1976 | Korea | Additional U.S. forces were sent to the demilitarized zone after two U.S. servicemen were shot and killed by North Korean troops while cutting down a tree. |
| May 19-June 1978 | Zaire | U.S. military transport aircraft were ordered to assist Belgian and French rescue operations in Zaire. |
| August 19, 1981 | Libya | U.S. planes based on the aircraft carrier Nimitz shot down two Libyan jets over the Gulf of Sidra after one of the Libyan jets fired a heat seeking missile. |
| March 18, 1983 | Egypt | U.S. AWACS were sent to Egypt when the Egyptians requested assistance in the wake of a Libyan bombing of a city in Sudan. |
| June 5, 1984 | Persian Gulf | Two Iranian fighter planes are shot down by Saudi Arabian jet fighters with the assistance of U.S. AWACS intelligence. |
| October 10, 1985 | Achille Lauro | Navy jets intercepted an Egyptian airliner, forcing it to land in Sicily. The plane was carrying the hijackers of the cruise ship Achille Lauro who had killed an American passenger. |
| July 14, 1986 | Bolivia | U.S. army personnel and equipment were sent to Bolivia to help that government fight drug traffickers. |

Table 8.2 (continued)

| March–<br>April 1988 | Panama | An additional 1900 American troops were sent to Panama to fortify American strength in the face of the increasing instability of the Noriega regime. |
| January 4, 1989 | Mediterranean<br>Sea | Two Libyan jet fighters are shot down by U.S. Navy F-14 fighter planes. |
| 1981–Present | El<br>Salvador | U.S. military "advisors" are sent to El Salvador to assist that government and military in its civil war against the FMLN. |

Source: Adapted from Collier, 1988, 1990.

The congressional lack of will to assert itself in decisions concerning war powers repeatedly eroded the legitimacy of the congressional threat and, consequently, the executive incentive to consult with Congress. During the airlifts of Danang and Saigon in April 1975, for example, although President Ford did not report to Congress under section 4(1)(a) of the resolution, there was a clear opportunity for Congress to enact legislation either authorizing the use of American forces or denying such authorization. Though he criticized Ford's lack of compliance with the War Powers Resolution in this instance, Zablocki admits, "...the failure of Congress to enact special legislative authority seemed to compromise its power in the commission of troops through joint legislative-executive action, thereby undermining full War Powers Resolution compliance" (Zablocki, 1984, 583).

Though President Ford did report the use of force to free the crew of the *Mayaguez*, a U.S. merchant ship which had been captured by the Cambodian navy, even citing section 4(a)(1), the report came to Congress after the decision to use force had been made but before the action had begun. While this represented an improvement over reports which failed to cite 4(a)(1), Franck and Weisband argue that the report "conduced not one whit to congressional codetermination of whether, when, or how to use force" (Franck and Weisband, 1979, 71).

As can be seen in Tables 8.1 and 8.2 this pattern continued through the Carter Administration, which at least acknowledged that Congress had a legitimate roll in foreign policy, and the Reagan Administration which fought congressional meddling all the way.

When Congress did finally exert itself in war powers, over the use of American troops in the Multinational Forces in Lebanon, it was only by way of compromise with the president. In exchange for invoking the time limit under subsection 4(a)(1) of the War Powers Resolution Congress agreed to extend authorization for the use of troops in Lebanon for an additional 18 months (the Multinational Forces in Lebanon Resolution) (Zablocki, 1984; Collier, 1988). In addition, the resolution authorized the president to take "such protective measures as may be necessary to ensure the safety of the Multinational Force in Lebanon" (*CQ Weekly Report*, October 8, 1983, 2101; Crabb and Holt, 1981, 146). This typically vague language gave the president enormous latitude of action.

While some viewed this episode as an example of congressional assertion in war powers (Zablocki, 1984; Sullivan, 1987) it is probably better characterized as yet another example of executive dominance. Though he signed the Multinational Forces in Lebanon Resolution, President Reagan still denied that his signature implied his agreement with the constitutionality or legitimacy of Congress' role:

> I do not and cannot cede any of the authority vested in me under the Constitution as President and as Commander-In-Chief of the United States Armed Forces. Nor should my signing be viewed as any acknowledgment that the president's constitutional authority can be impermissibly infringed by statute, that congressional authorization would be required if and when the period specified in ...the War Powers Resolution might be deemed to have been triggered and the period had expired, or that [the eighteen month authorization] may be interpreted to revise the President's constitutional authority to deploy United States Armed Forces (*CQ Weekly Report*, October 15, 1983, 2142).

Congress had the power to invoke the time limit under 4(a)(1) without striking a deal with the president, even if the reason for invoking the limit was merely to extend it. But instead of taking the positive action (which Congress so often laments it is blocked from doing by the executive) Congress once more hid behind the cloak of executive leadership. For the executive's part, Reagan was able to garner formal congressional support for action which, after the death of the two Marines in August 1983, was growing increasingly controversial. Moreover, this support came on the eve of an election year and at very little cost to the president since he ceded nothing as to the legitimacy of Congress' role.

Still, Congress' goal was achieved: it could now claim to have been "a part" of the decision making process over Lebanon. As constitutional scholar Michael Glennon commented, "In the face of administration truculence...Congress' response carried all the logic of a homeowner's allowing an arsonist to torch his house so as to avoid the humiliation of having it done without his consent" (Glennon, 1984, 667).

Congress had no way of knowing at the time how fateful the extended authorization would be, as 241 Marines were soon to be killed in a terrorist bombing on their base. In this instance, the president was more than happy to share responsibility for U.S. policy with the legislature.

In a few instances legislators sought to redress executive noncompliance with the War Powers Resolution through court action. In the case of U.S. troops in El Salvador, for example, Congressman George Crockett of Michigan and 10 other representatives filed suit in the U.S. District Court of D.C. challenging the executive action (*Crockett v. Reagan*, 588 F. Supp. 839 [D.C. 1982]). A similar case was brought by members of the House of Representatives seeking to force President Reagan to report on the involvement of American troops in the Persian Gulf under section 4(a)(1) (*Lowry v. Reagan*, 676 F. Supp. 333 [D.D.C. 1987]). Most recently members of Congress attempted to file suit against the massive deployment of troops in Saudi Arabia following the Iraqi invasion of Kuwait. In each of these cases the court relied on the "political question doctrine" to rule that the case was nonjusticiable.

These rulings, however, have proven curious in light of the Supreme Court's willingness to hand down such a broad ruling in the *Chadha* case, going well beyond the ruling necessary merely to dispose of the question of executive versus legislative authority in immigration policy (Glennon, 1984, 1990). The text of that ruling argues,

> the presence of constitutional issues with significant political overtones does not automatically invoke the political question doctrine. Resolution of litigation challenging the constitutional authority of one of the three branches cannot be evaded by courts because the issues have political implications (*INS v. Chadha*, 462 U.S. 919, 942-943 [1983], see also Ely, 1988, 1364).

Indeed, Ely suggests that the political questions doctrine "was never more than a congeries of excuses for not deciding issues otherwise properly brought before the court...[It] is like the Holy Roman Empire. It doesn't have much to do with whether the question is "political" in any ordinary sense" (Ely, 1988, 1364).

The ambivalence in public opinion which surrounded the decision to use force against Iraq to "liberate" Kuwait presented Congress with a unique opportunity in the post-war period to preempt American military action before it had begun. (This is not to say that it should have, merely that it might have). Though in the end Congress voted to approve authorization to use force the vote was close and many members opposed the president. The political fallout of this opposition in the next election cycle could well determine whether American politics is seeing the beginnings of a new era of congressional latitude on issues of war and peace or, in the event of a political backlash, a lesson that the old standards of rallying 'round the president still apply.

In either event, as the debate revealed, members of Congress were initially most concerned with the *means* by which the president unilaterally decided to deploy such a massive force in the Persian Gulf. Though the administration argued that the need for quick action to prevent Saddam Hussein's further expansion into Saudi Arabia came at a time when Congress was in summer recess, many in Congress saw it as yet another attempt to evade consultation. At the same time, however, the majority of members expressed support for the overall policy. Later, as the January 15 U.N. deadline authorizing the international coalition's use of force drew near, Congress vocally opposed both the lack of congressional consultation and the substance of U.S. policy. Many felt that international sanctions against Iraq should be given a longer chance to work.

President Bush repeatedly argued that if Congress could not support him in authorizing the use of force against Iraq, he would not request their permission. As had his predecessors, Bush was adamant that his powers as president and commander-in-chief justified his actions.

In the end, Congress, reflecting the split in public opinion, voted by a narrow margin to authorize American participation in the use of force against Iraq (*Los Angeles Times*, January 13, 1991, A10). Whether this vote symbolizes the beginnings of greater acceptance of congressional disagreement with the president in times of crisis, or merely an anomaly inspired by ambivalent public opinion will be critical in guiding similar congressional votes in the future.

## Conclusion

The comments of Rep. Clement Zablocki (D-Wisc.), a sponsor of the War Powers Resolution, sum up one of the major reasons for congressional lack of will. "Congress could have been more determined in its oversight of executive branch compliance," he admits.

> The principle reason for this inadequate oversight lies in the political dynamics surrounding the various tests of compliance....Each action was politically popular when it was taken, of short duration, and involved objectives which overshadowed concerns about the supposed technicalities of consultation and reporting under the War Powers Resolution. Achieving congressional consensus on a political strategy for

insuring executive compliance with the War Powers Resolution is difficult enough; under circumstances of politically popular short-term rescues of American citizens, it became impossible (Zablocki, 1984, 586-587).

It should be no surprise, therefore, that without the congressional will to enforce the limits on executive action potentially available in the War Powers Resolution, executives have shown little inclination to bring Congress in as a codeterminor of foreign policy, particularly in such a critical area as war powers. As Glennon argues, "Presidents...cannot reasonably be expected to cede to the Congress any greater role in the decision making process than the Congress *legitimately* and *clearly* demands" (emphasis original) (Glennon, 1984, 660).

Though the statutory provisions of the War Powers Resolution held the potential of significantly readjusting the balance of decision-making power between the executive and legislature, in the end they proved feeble. Without the institutional *and* individual will to enforce the withdrawal of troops Congress had little hope of compelling the president to engage in significant consultation before deciding on a military course of action. As for the legislative veto, the subject was seldom even raised.

Though Congress' real aim was to ensure its institutional position as a partner in war powers decision making, it could not regain this status without a credible threat that it might reverse executive policy. The political cost of taking such an action, however, reduced that threat to mere posturing. The loss of the legislative veto, therefore, has had little effect on congressional-executive relations in war powers. Though conflict remains between the branches on this issue, the availability of statutory leverage is irrelevant without the political will to exercise its use. This will was not present before the *Chadha* decision nor after it.

In the end, the true value of the War Powers Resolution was symbolic rather than statutory (Scheidt, 1987, 8; Sullivan, 1987).

# 9

---

# Toward an Effective Policy Process

When contemplating the relationship between Congress and the president in foreign policy one must keep in mind that the postwar bipartisan consensus and general congressional acquiescence has been the historical exception rather than rule. And as we move farther and farther from the conditions which sustained such a relationship, it is unproductive to seek solutions to current policy problems which attempt to put the genie back in the bottle and return Congress to a subservient role. As Jentleson has argued, "A substantial role for Congress in U.S. international diplomacy is a given. It is that point from which all serious discussion about how to make the process work better should begin" (Jentleson, 1990, 197). The issue at hand, then, is not *whether* but *how* to forge a workable accommodation between the branches.

In a period of international transition, a period in which 50 years of Cold War has suddenly given way to revolutionary changes in Eastern Europe, the former Soviet Union, and the world, the ability of the United States to maintain an effective, forward-looking foreign policy is of critical importance. Over the next few decades the primary issues in foreign affairs are likely be economic rather than military. Finesse and diplomacy will displace force and bluster. In such a world it will be critical to present ourselves as a cohesive and stable partner in international dealings.

With the demise of the postwar foreign policy consensus has come an unravelling of American foreign policy coherence. Instead of a decision-making process based upon an overall design with distinct goals, we now see a series of outcomes determined by which branch (Congress or the executive) is able to get "one up" on the other. Though he was writing in a period of relative policy coherence, Neustadt's description of congressional-executive jousting over policy is apt: "The stage is set for that great game, much like collective bargaining, in which each side seeks to profit from the other's needs and fears. It is a game played catch-as-catch-can, case by case" (Neustadt, 1960, 45-46).

Each side has tools at its disposal with which it can pressure (often embarrass) the other into compromise or capitulation. Though the president's tools are generally stronger, Congress retains the ability to fight, and if it can't win it can at least delay, dispute or deride executive policy proposals enough to effectively undermine domestic and international confidence in the conviction behind American policy. Though interbranch conflict cannot, and should not, be completely eliminated, what is needed is a policy process wherein conflict can be managed and turned to constructive use.

It may be difficult for Americans to recognize just how damaging high profile policy battles are to the international perception of the credibility of the president and the coherence of American policy. One recent event which may help to shed some perspective on the effects of such battles was the 1991 Philippines Senate vote to defeat President Corazon Aquino's agreement with the United States for the continued leasing of the Subic Bay Naval Base. This public rejection of Aquino's initiative was not only embarrassing for both the Philippines and the United States, but brought into serious question the standing of Aquino and her ability to ensure the reliability of agreements which she negotiated. The same is true when the U.S. Congress publicly chastises the president over foreign policy.

This is not to argue that the president should have a free hand and that Congress should remain silent. It *is* to argue that policy disagreement is an inherent part of our type of government but that conflict must be resolved in a discreet manner in order to avoid the fundamental damage which it can do to the U.S. reputation abroad.

At home, the high profile battles between Congress and the president create an atmosphere of hostility and mistrust which may feed into other policy areas. The practice of retaliation for one policy by holding another hostage, perhaps through appropriations restrictions, inaction or counter-legislation is well established. Thus, increased conflict in foreign policy can have detrimental effects across the spectrum of interbranch relations, undermining the entire process of effective governance. Developing a political accommodation for the formulation of foreign policy, therefore, will have beneficial ramifications in the domestic as well as foreign policy arenas.

The main issue raised in this work is not whether Congress and the president *should* work together on foreign policy. As Sundquist concedes, "almost everybody, at both ends of Pennsylvania Avenue, now endorses the general objective of consultation" (Sundquist, 1981, 303). The real question is what happens when Congress fundamentally opposes the president? How, then, do the statutory tools available to Congress come into play to either exacerbate conflict or invite cooperation and compromise?

## Why We Didn't See It Coming

Though the post-war bipartisan consensus in foreign policy has generally been evoked to explain the relative comity between Congress and the executive, especially in the 1950s, the unifying role of consultation should not be overlooked. An example from the Truman Administration is illustrative. Though the Republican-controlled Congress did not publicly oppose Truman on the Truman Doctrine, NATO, or the Marshall Plan, it did raise vocal objections to his policy of non-intervention when Mao emerged victorious in the Chinese Revolution. A major difference among these instances is that Truman had consulted Congress on the former, but did not consult over China (Destler, Gelb and Lake 1984). The lid on conflict has historically been very loose, but in the immediate postwar period, due largely to the consensus in foreign policy, as long as some degree of consultation was undertaken cooperation could be achieved. When the foreign policy consensus broke down, however, consultation became the exception. The legislative veto provided the mechanism to compel consultation when it was needed the most: in the absence of policy agreement.

The irony of the *Chadha* decision is that it has ultimately served to clarify for us just how important the legislative veto really was in forging interbranch policy accommodation in foreign policy. In cases of policy disagreement between Congress and the executive, it allowed the *process* of policy formulation to move forward by creating a context in which it was in the interests of each branch to cooperate and, at times, even compromise with the other. Though the legislative veto did not eliminate the interbranch conflict which has been pervasive in the last two decades, it did serve as a unique tool to mitigate and diffuse disagreements before they became high profile, public battles.

Given the disproportionate use of legislative veto provisions in domestic legislation, it is not surprising that analyses and predictions concerning the impact which *Chadha* would have focussed primarily on executive agencies and the bureaucracy. But in doing so, scholars failed to recognize the significant differences between domestic and foreign policy making which would affect the post-*Chadha* policy process.

First of all, a relatively even power balance between the institutions in the process of domestic policy making made the legislative veto a mutually beneficial instrument. (Though not all players saw it that way all of the time). The number of informal legislative veto agreements between congressional committees and executive agencies even after *Chadha* (Fisher, 1987) is testimony to the mutual benefits which resulted from the statutory accommodation. In foreign policy, by contrast, the postwar dominance of the executive branch and broad claims of authority to serve as the "sole organ of the federal government in international relations" belie expectations of executive cooperation unless coerced. The loss of the legislative veto removed the most viable source of coercion which Congress had. It changed the calculations of executive action, from the incentive to consult and compromise to the incentive to face down congressional opposition. Leverage in policy disputes shifted once again toward the executive who could prevail with only one-third plus one vote in either house--a tally not hard to achieve when the president lobbies his partisans.

Another critical difference between domestic and foreign policy is the level at which most policy is decided. Where most domestic policy disagreements are resolved through "low politics" (committee-agency interaction), foreign policy disputes tend to become "high politics," involving the president himself and his senior policy advisors. Again, the nature of the conflict makes compromise inherently difficult as the prestige of the president and his international reputation are involved.

But the theoretical argument advanced in this work does have implications for domestic policy as well as foreign policy. The lesson is that statutory tools matter, and this is true across the board. The ability to create a policy process which works, one which allows policy formulation to proceed in a constructive manner despite policy disagreements, relies on the selection of the proper statutory tools. The tools are available to create an incentive structure in which both parties (Congress and the executive) see their interests served by consultation and compromise. The attendant requirement, however, is that Congress be willing to take more responsibility for, and be more accountable for, the policies which are created.

## Constructive v. Destructive Conflict

Conflict between the branches is not inherently bad. Indeed, our system of governing institutions was set up precisely to inspire a degree of conflict and tension which would serve to check and balance the powers of each branch vis-a-vis the others. But there must be a distinction made between constructive and destructive conflict; between the types of policy debates which inject prudent consideration of diverse alternatives and ensure representation, and the kind which undermine the stability and coherence of policy and leave a perception of unreliability in the international arena.

Probably the most obvious benefit of conflict in foreign policy is the leverage which the threat of congressional opposition gives the president when trying to convince another country to undertake a particular course of action. Often referred to as the "good cop, bad cop" scenario, by raising the specter of congressional opposition, the president can often induce compromise from a foreign government in the effort to make a policy more acceptable to Congress. Ultimately the interests of the United States can be served by such manipulation. A case in point is China's recent declaration of its intention to become a signatory to the U.N. Treaty on the Non-Proliferation of Nuclear Weapons, probably in the effort to stave off congressional opposition to the renewal of its MFN trade status (which the president supports).

But the advantages of the "good cop, bad cop" scenario do not outweigh the destructive impact which *excessive* interbranch conflict has on American foreign policy. Much of interbranch conflict is as much the result of institutional turf wars as of substantive policy disagreement (Warburg, 1989). The sense that Congress has been left out of the policy process is a major contributor to the fray. There are, of course, fundamental disagreements concerning the substance of policy, but these are often so basic that foreign governments refuse to compromise in what they see as capitulation to their adversaries. Arab governments' refusals to recognize and negotiate with Israel under U.N. resolutions 242 and 338 are cases in point.

There are a number of instances in which congressional obstruction of executive policy plans can be shown to have served the national interest and averted a serious foreign policy blunder. The sale of AWACS to Iran in the mid-70s provides a prime (if serendipitous) example. Congressional pressure to withdraw from Vietnam, opposition to American military involvement in Central America, and insistence upon sanctions against South Africa provide further evidence. But the effort to reform the relationship between Congress and the president in foreign policy cannot find its foundation in examples of policy success through codetermination. Assessments of this type are inherently subjective. While one observer may call the prevention of military involvement in Nicaragua or El Salvador a success, another may call it a serious mistake. The sanctions against South Africa may have been the moral course of action to one person, and an immoral and naive policy to another.

Recommendations for reform must focus on the policy *process* rather than policy outcomes. Though the substance of policy is not irrelevant, this must be left to the political forces of the time. A sound policy process will accommodate debate, diverse opinions and compromise which in the end will determine the outcome of policy. But more importantly, a sound process will avoid the destructive conflict which is so evident in much of the current formulation of policy.


## The Incentive to Cooperate

Just how relations between the branches can be formulated to reduce conflict and improve the efficiency and coherence of policy has long been a source of debate (Sundquist, 1981). Suggestions have ranged from total structural reform of the governing institutions (Elliott, 1935) to creating a joint council between the cabinet and legislative leaders (Corwin, 1957; Corwin and Koenig, 1956) to creating a more responsible party system (E.E. Schattschneider, 1950).

But many of these suggestions, appealing as they may be, would require major changes to the current system. Though that may be exactly what is needed, in practice they are difficult to implement. Inertia is a powerful thing. So are vested interests. Some more practical alternatives are available *within* the current system. But the bad news is that the same factors which work against comity in current relationships make the adoption of some of these alternatives problematic.

Most recent studies of foreign policy lament the degenerating relationship between Congress and the president, note the destructive effects that struggles have on the reputation and effectiveness of American foreign policy, and end with the standard plea for more cooperation between the branches. But there must be more. Madison knew that there was little hope in relying upon the altruism or reasoned restraint of the nation's governors to work together for the greater good, and there is little reason to expect any differently today. What is needed is to reconstruct a system of incentives and disincentives so that, as Madison had argued, our governors would do the right thing in spite of themselves.

I have argued that the loss of the legislative veto has led Congress to adopt means which ignite greater conflict in the effort to affect foreign policy. But there are other options which Congress could have turned to, one of which would have had virtually the same effect as the legislative veto. The problem as legislators see it, however, is that the alternatives would require Congress to take a greater degree of responsibility for policy. In keeping with their overall risk-aversion, they have been reluctant to seriously consider these options. But given the problems inherent in the current relationship between the branches, it is time to take another look.

One option is to include provisions for joint resolutions of *approval* in legislation pertaining to those issues which, as revealed in the typology as well as the experience of legislators, are likely to cause serious conflict between Congress and the president. Strategic-salient issues like arms sales to the Middle East or intermestic issues such as most-favored-nation trade status are the likely suspects (see also Hamilton and Van Dusen, 1978).

The joint resolution of approval requires that both houses of Congress give affirmative votes to any legislation before it can be enacted into law. It is subject to presidential veto, and as such does not violate constitutional lawmaking procedures. By requiring both houses to approve any proposal this statutory tool effectively lays the responsibility for forging a consensus on the executive. Since failure to garner support in either house would kill the initiative, the joint resolution of approval affords Congress the leverage of the legislative veto without the constitutionally dubious complications.

More importantly, the joint resolution of approval recreates an incentive structure conducive to cooperation between the branches. Recognizing the real danger of defeat if congressional opposition is not reconciled, the executive finds its own interests at risk. The incentive is to reconcile conflict by consulting with opponents *before* legislation reaches a vote. As with the legislative veto, the joint resolution of approval does not eliminate conflict. What it does is to provide a means to resolve that conflict in a discrete fashion rather than a public battle.

Joint resolution of approval provisions are not unknown to legislators; indeed a fair number can be found in legislation, particularly in the domestic arena. But in foreign policy legislators have been reluctant to adopt joint resolutions of approval as a means of influence because they fear that it will increase the already burdened workload of Congress. While it is true that the joint resolution of approval would require congressional action, it is not necessarily the case that the workload involved would be any greater than what exists today. The recommendation is that the joint resolution of approval be included in those issue areas which are likely to inspire a high degree of conflict, not across the board. In cases of strong policy disagreement *and* congressional willingness to oppose the president, legislators' workloads are already increased as the battle ensues. With the resolution of approval, it may even be the case that their workloads would decrease, since it would be in the interests of the executive branch to provide legislators with issue information in the effort to gain support. Clearly legislators will want independent sources of information, and will get them both from lobby groups and from the resources available to Congress in the Congressional Research Service. In addition, the work formerly involved in garnering support for opposing executive policy will be reduced, since the burden would shift to the president to *gain* support.

Legislators are always wary of putting themselves in a position of responsibility or accountability for policy. Blame-avoidance is the great congressional pastime. The joint resolution of approval threatens legislators with accountability since a failed policy can be traced back to explicit congressional approval. In this sense, the joint resolution of *dis*approval's appeal is that it allows legislators to avoid blame since policies are killed by congressional action but can be implemented by congressional *in*action. A failed policy, therefore, can be plausibly denied by Congress since they are never forced to explicitly endorse it.

But where the joint resolution of disapproval has high potential for conflict and ultimately low potential for policy influence, the joint resolution of *approval* holds just the opposite--low potential for conflict and high potential for policy influence. If Congress wants to retake a substantial institutional role in foreign policy, legislators are going to have to accept some degree of responsibility. And remember, the policies which Congress will be approving will also be those which the executive has initiated. If one assumes that the president will only initiate policies which he himself supports, then it is highly unlikely that the issue of a veto would ever arise in the event that a joint resolution of *approval* is passed. Rather than taking the blame, this allows Congress both to share in the policy making process and to claim credit for successful policies.

Another option to decrease the degree of conflict between the branches is to return to an informal legislative veto agreement. In issue areas where the executive recognizes the likelihood of conflict (and its destructive potential) an agreement could be worked out whereby the committee(s) who are dealing with appropriations for a given policy would retain the prerogative to rescind authority for an appropriation in the event that it does not approve of the use of funds. While this sounds like the legislative veto which was struck down in *Chadha*, it is not. It's constitutionality rests on the fact that the veto power would pertain only to internal workings of Congress, not "the legal rights, duties and relations of persons" outside the legislative branch (which the Court ruled unconstitutional) (Fisher, 1987, 426). In fact, a precedent has been set for this type of informal legislative veto agreement in foreign policy in an accommodation between the Bush Administration and Congress on the issue of aid to the Contras. Informal agreements of this type could go a long way in the search for cooperation between Congress and the president.

The problem with this sort of recommendation is that it relies heavily upon some degree of pre-existing comity between the branches. That is, it presumes that the executive is willing to allow Congress a degree of leverage in policy in return for at least temporary flexibility. As I have argued in this work, however, the incentive for the executive branch is generally to make an "end run" on Congress, facing down opposition *without* compromise in the relative certainty of ultimate success. In order for compromises and accommodations (such as that made over aid to the Contras) to succeed, both branches must recognize the destructive influence which their actions are having on foreign policy and be committed to alleviating it.

### The Limits of Statutory Solutions

The goal of implementing the suggested reforms is not to make Congress the dominant institution in foreign policy. It is neither practical nor, probably, desirable for the Congress to take the lead in international affairs. Indeed, few, if any, members of that institution would argue today for that role. The advantages of executive leadership remain. The enduring benefits which come from the hierarchical structure of the executive branch, its informational resources, and capacity for quick action when necessary remain critical to an effective foreign policy. In addition, the traditional (and constitutional) role of the executive as the focal point of diplomacy facilitates international relations.

The goal, rather, is to bring Congress back into the policy making process in a manner which was intended by the framers of the Constitution without reintroducing the disadvantages which the eighteenth century structure created for twentieth century circumstances. Congress is not going to revert to the acquiescent junior partner which it was prior to the 1970s. At the same time, the 50 year history of executive dominance in foreign policy will not simply melt away. The executive is not only logistically better equipped to carry out the day-to-day foreign policy needs of the country, but has become the symbol of the nation in international relations both for its own citizens and to other countries. So while Congress will remain the junior partner, it will insist upon a substantive role in policy formulation.

Creating the incentive for consultation does not resolve the problems of congressional obstructionism or aversion to take responsibility for policy. These remain problems which only legislators themselves can solve. If representatives are determined to torpedo executive policy initiatives without offering constructive alternatives, no statutory alternatives will stop them. But in most instances legislators are as committed to a successful foreign policy as the executive is. The obstructionism which has resulted in the past was often catalyzed by resentment over executive resistance to take the congressional role in the policy process seriously. By inducing consultation and compromise through alternative statutory tools, Congress can fulfill its original intentions of delegating policy making authority to the executive while retaining a genuine oversight capability.

Another cautionary note must be sounded concerning the effect of statutory alternatives (such as the joint resolution of approval or informal legislative veto agreements) on the ability of special interest groups to gain undue leverage over policy. Taking a lesson from domestic policy, one could argue that by giving what amounts to veto power to Congress or congressional committees, we would also be giving veto power to powerful lobby groups who have a vested interest in foreign policy and significant leverage over legislators.

This is a very real consideration and one which should be guarded against. But there are also a few factors distinguishing foreign policy from domestic policy which may reduce the danger of undue leverage for special interests. First, foreign policy is generally higher in profile than is much of domestic policy. The committee-agency-interest group "iron triangles" so common in domestic policy are more rare in foreign policy because executive policy is not made at the agency level. It generally involves high level State Department officials and often the president himself. This is particularly true of the issues which tend to promote interbranch conflict, and precisely the issues in which joint resolutions of approval or informal legislative vetoes would be used. Thus the ability of special interests to muscle legislators would be undermined by the profile of the issue.

Secondly, where the powerful interest groups lobbying on foreign policy issues were once restricted to the Israeli or Greek lobbies, today there are many more, and many more powerful interest groups (Jentleson, 1990; Mann, 1990). Given the intricate and tangled web of international power balances, policy toward one country is likely to be watched closely by its neighbors and/or adversaries. Whereas in much of domestic policy (especially regulatory) legislation affects highly specialized interest groups and is consequently of little interest to other groups, in foreign policy the interested parties will be of a broader spectrum. Again, the prospects of specialized interest groups gaining undue leverage over committees dealing with foreign policy is undermined by the profile of the issues.

Finally, the process of consultation itself must be effective and regularized. As Mann has argued, "mechanisms for consultation can be effective only insofar as those being consulted can speak for the full Congress" (Mann, 1990, 31-32). Compelling consultation with Congress, only to have an unorganized method or require the input of all 535 members would undermine the validity of the process. The consultation process must not be an excessive burden to the executive (undermining the incentive to consult) but must be a reasonable exercise.

Ideally, the consultative committee of Congress would include an array of party leaders, and committee and subcommittee members whose jurisdictions entail the foreign policy issues in question. By including a mixture of senior and junior representatives from across the ideological spectrum the prospects for effective coalition building are enhanced. Legislators themselves have a critical role to play by reducing committee and subcommittee rivalries over jurisdictions so that the consultation process can work effectively and efficiently.

If Congress wants a serious role in the formulation of American foreign policy there are statutory means to achieve it. Doing so, however, would require Congress to take a more responsible role than it has heretofore been willing to take--responsible both in terms of accountability for policy, and in terms of leaving its obstructionist bad habits behind.

## Conclusion

Though the Constitution left significant confusion as to the proper roles of Congress and the executive in the formulation of contemporary American foreign policy, there is the potential for effective political accommodation. The *Chadha* decision dissolved one such attempt. In its aftermath Congressional Research Service Council Mort Rosenberg has predicted, a "lengthy period of legal trench warfare" awaits as Congress and the president continue to battle over foreign affairs (*CQ Almanac*, Feb. 3, 1990, 295). If the branches are unable to forge a new political accommodation, he is probably right.

But what the *Chadha* decision put asunder, the Congress itself could resurrect. That is, to create a structure in which it is in the president's clear interests to consult and compromise with Congress on those issues in which Congress has the incentive and the will to seriously oppose his policies.   As it stands, the rational course for the president is to face down Congress, ride out the objections and fiery rhetoric which their disputes inspire, and hold firm to policy proposals while lobbying partisans (particularly in the Senate).   Following this process the president's policy is almost certain to prevail, in spite of the destructive impact such an embattled process has on American foreign policy.

But Congress has the power to change this.  It has the statutory tools to remodel the structure of incentives which the executive faces.   As Napoleon said, "The tools belong to the man who can use them."  What Congress needs to find is the fortitude to accept a higher degree of responsibility for policy and the insight to use its weapons wisely.

# Notes

1.  Foreign Policy legislation allowing annulment by concurrent resolution includes: War Powers Resolution (1973); Amendments to the Mineral Leasing Act of 1920 (1973); Department of Defense Authorizations (1974); Foreign Assistance Act (1974); International Broadcasting Board Authorization (1975); Sinai Early Warning System Agreement Resolution (1975); International Security Assistance and Arms Export Control Act (1976); Export Administration Amendments (1977); International Navigational Rules Act (1977); International Security Assistance Act (1977); Nuclear Non-Proliferation Act (1978); Outer Continental Shelf Lands Act Amendments (1978); International Security Assistance Act (1978).

Foreign Policy legislation allowing annulment by single-house veto includes: International Development and Food Assistance Act (1975); International Development and Food Assistance Act (1978).

Foreign Policy legislation requiring reporting to Congress includes: Foreign Assistance Appropriations Act (1970); Foreign Assistance Act (1972); Export-Import Bank Act Amendments (1977). Legislation Requiring reporting to Congressional Committees includes: Foreign Assistance Act (1973); Foreign Assistance Appropriations (1974); Trade Act (1975); Foreign Assistance Appropriations (1975); Foreign Relations Authorization (1975); International Development and Food Assistance Act (1977); Foreign Assistance and Related Programs Appropriations Act (1977); Agricultural Trade Act (1978); Foreign Intelligence Surveillance Act (1978).

2.  22 U.S.C. 2776; PL 90-629, 82 Stat. 1320, Sec. 36(b).

3.  The term "sole organ" was actually borrowed from part of a speech made by Justice John Marshall to the House of Representatives over a hundred years earlier (see Glennon, 1990, 8.)

4.  The types of vetoes considered in this work are restricted to those which could be undertaken unilaterally by Congress and did not allow for Presidential recourse. These are what Cooper (1985) terms "congressional" forms of the veto. Other authors also include report-and-wait provisions and joint resolutions, what Cooper calls "law" forms of the veto, under the general term of "legislative veto." While it is true that "law" forms provide a means for Congress to nullify executive action, these means are not constitutionally questionable and were not affected by the *Chadha* decision. The "law" forms provide the most feasible alternatives to "congressional" forms of the veto.

5.  *Process Gas Consumers Group v. Consumer Energy Council* and *United States Senate v. FTC*. The logic of these two rulings, along with *Chadha* left little doubt that the committee form of the veto or any mixed forms was also considered unconstitutional.

6.  Taking 1977 as the beginning year for the quantiative analysis eliminates the Watergate and Vietnam years in which an unusual degree of interbranch conflict may distort the data. These years are discussed, however, in the qualitative case studies. For this measure the year 1990 has not been included because the major source of information, the Congressional Research Service Digest of General Public Bills and Resolutions has not yet been compiled nor have many of the relevant Committee Calendars. It should be noted that the Digest for 1989 is also unavailable. Although Committee Calendars and the Congressional Record Index are available for 1989, estimates for this year are likely to remain underestimated. The Digest has generally been found to be more comprehensive than both of these other sources combined for the years under study, though supplements are still useful.

7.  For an extremely interesting and well documented account of the two and one half year battle over the Jackson-Vanik Amendment to the Trade Act of 1974 see Stern's *Water's Edge* (1979).

8.  The "education tax" for emigres from the Soviet Union ranged anywhere from $5,000 to $30,000.

9.  The case *Cranston v. Reagan* was ultimately ruled nonjusticiable by the court on the grounds that it was a political and not a judicial matter (the "political questions" doctrine).

10.  Expressing amazement at the administration's seemingly inexhaustible ability to find reasons for maintaining U.S. aid to Pakistan, one Senate staffer mused: "After the Afghanistan situation ended, then it was the need to protect the fragile flower of democracy embodied in Benazir Bhutto. And then when she was gone, then critics pointed to Pakistani troops in the Middle East and argued that we don't want to stab our loyal ally in the back!"

11.  Constitutional scholar Louis Fisher argues that in fact the *Chadha* decision does not apply to the War Powers Resolution since Congress never delegated any authority to the executive through the legislation. As such, he argues, the legislative veto was never "lost" in War Powers and its provisions remain constitutional (Fisher, 1991).

12.  The *Chadha* decision was reaffirmed by the D.C. Court of Appeals which struck down the validity of the concurrent resolution in a case challenging the Federal Trade Commission Improvements Act of 1980 (*Process Gas Consumers Group v. Consumer Energy Council*, 463, U.S. 1216 [1983]). It was this decision,

even more than the actual *Chadha* case (which struck down the one-house veto) which directly applies to 5(c) of War Powers.

# References

Aberbach, Joel. 1990. *Keeping A Watchful Eye: The Politics of Congressional Oversight.* Washington, D.C.: The Brookings Institution.

Acheson, Dean. 1969. *Present at the Creation: My Years at the State Department.* New York: W.W. Norton & Company.

Ambrose, Stephen. 1988. *Rise To Globalism: American Foreign Policy Since 1938* Fifth Edition. New York: Penguin Books.

Baker, Steven. 1984. "Nuclear Nonproliferation," in H. Purvis and S. Baker, eds. *Legislating Foreign Policy.* Pp. 136-159. Boulder: Westview Press.

"Both Parties Have Big Stake in Vote." 1991. *Los Angeles Times*, January 13, A10.

"Brazil and Argentina Ban Production and Testing of Nuclear Weapons." *Los Angeles Times*, November 28, 1990.

Bruff, Harold and Ernest Gellhorn. 1977. "Congressional Control of Administrative Regulation: A Study of Legislative Vetoes." *Harvard Law Review* 90: 1369-1440.

Burns, James MacGregor. 1984. *The Power to Lead: The Crisis of the American Presidency.* New York: Simon and Schuster.

Bush, George. 1989. Presidential Statement: Veto of Chinese Immigration Relief. The White House. November 30.

Caldwell, Dan. 1981. "The Jackson-Vanik Amendment," in J. Spanier and J. Nogee, eds., *Congress, the Presidency and American Foreign Policy.* Pp. 1-12. New York: Pergamon Press.

Carter, Jimmy. 1978. *Public Papers of the Presidents: Jimmy Carter* 1. Washington D.C.: Government Printing Office.

_____. 1979. *Public Papers of the Presidents: Jimmy Carter* 1. Washington, D.C.: Government Printing Office.

Cassidy, Stephen. 1989. "The Newest Member of the Nuclear Club: Pakistan's Drive For A Nuclear Weapons Capability and United States Nuclear Nonproliferation Policy." *Hastings International and Comparative Law Review* 12: 679-734.

"China Agrees To Sign Global Nuclear Treaty." 1991. *Los Angeles Times*, August 11, A1.

Choper, Jesse H. 1980. *Judicial Review and the National Political Process: A Functional Reconsideration of the Role of the Supreme Court.* Chicago: The University of Chicago Press.

Clark, Donald. 1986. "Nuclear Nonproliferation Legislation After Chadha: Nonjusticiable Political Questions and the Loss of the Legislative Veto." *Syracuse Law Review* 37: 899-917.

Collier, Ellen C. 1988. "The War Powers Resolution: Fifteen Years of Experience." CRS Report For Congress. August 3. Washington, D.C.: Congressional Research Service.

_____. 1990. War Powers Resolution: Presidential Compliance. CRS Issue Brief. August 29. Washington, D.C.: Congressional Research Service.

Collier, Ellen, Richard Grimmett, Larry Nowles and Warren Donnelly. 1984. "Foreign Policy Effects of the Supreme Court's Legislative Veto Decision." CRS Issue Brief. Washington, D.C.: Congressional Research Service.

*Congressional Quarterly Almanac.* Various years 1977-1987. Washington, D.C.: CQ Press.

*Congressional Quarterly Weekly Report.* 1989. "A Policy Confrontation on China?" June 24, Pp. 1564. Washington, D.C.: CQ Press.

*Congressional Quarterly Weekly Report.* 1989. "Aid For Chinese Students." July 15, Pp. 1787. Washington, D.C.: CQ Press.

*Congressional Quarterly Weekly Report.* 1990. "Bill Links China's MFN Status To Human Rights Progress." July 14, Pp. 2200-2201. Washington, D.C.: CQ Press.

*Congressional Quarterly Weekly Report.* 1989. "Brutal Crackdown in Beijing Deals Blow to U.S. Ties." June 10, Pp. 1411-1414. Washington, D.C.: CQ Press.

*Congressional Quarterly Weekly Report.* 1990. "Bush Lifts Soviet Credit Ban To Ease Food Shortage." 1990. December 15, Pp. 4144-4145. Washington, D.C.: CQ Press.

*Congressional Quarterly Weekly Report.* 1990. "Bush Renews MFN for China, Stirs Angry Hill Reaction." May 26, Pp. 1639. Washington, D.C.: CQ Press.

*Congressional Quarterly Weekly Report.* 1990. "Bush Throws Down the Gauntlet on Provisions He Opposes." 1990. January 24, Pp. 603-604. Washington, D.C.: CQ Press.

*Congressional Quarterly Weekly Report.* 1981. "Congress Appears Willing To Approve Aid To Pakistan." December 5, Pp. 2411-2414. Washington, D.C.: CQ Press.

*Congressional Quarterly Weekly Report.* 1990. "Congress Cuts Tariffs on Czech Imports." October 27, Pp. 3586. Washington, D.C.: CQ Press.

*Congressional Quarterly Weekly Report.* 1981. "Congress Requests Non-Proliferation Policy." July 25, Pp. 1348-1349. Washington, D.C.: CQ Press.

*Congressional Quarterly Weekly Report.* 1990. "GOP Senators Save Bush In China Veto Test." January 27, Pp. 245-246. Washington, D.C.: CQ Press.

*Congressional Quarterly Weekly Report.* 1989. "House Drops Return-Home Rule For Chinese Students Here." August 5, Pp. 2049. Washington, D.C.: CQ Press.

*Congressional Quarterly Weekly Report.* 1989. "House Panel Agrees to Shelter Chinese Students, Others." July 22, Pp. 1847. Washington, D.C.: CQ Press.

*Congressional Quarterly Weekly Report.* 1989. "House Stiffens Sanctions on China." July 1, Pp. 1624. Washington, D.C.: CQ Press.

*Congressional Quarterly Weekly Report.* 1989. "Hungary: Trade Concession Voted by House." September 9, Pp. 2325. Washington, D.C.: CQ Press.

*Congressional Quarterly Weekly Report.* 1983. "Joint Resolution To Keep Marines In Lebanon." October 8, Pp. 1201-1202. Washington, D.C.: CQ Press.

*Congressional Quarterly Weekly Report.* 1990. "Panel OKs China MFN Status, Seeks Future Rights Gains." July 21, Pp. 2288. Washington, D.C.: CQ Press.

*Congressional Quarterly Weekly Report.* 1981. "Reagan and Congress Review U.S. Efforts to Help Prevent U.S. Efforts To Help Prevent Nuclear Arms Proliferation." July 11. Pp. 1223-1228. Washington, D.C.: CQ Press.

*Congressional Quarterly Weekly Report.* 1983. "Resolution on Lebanon Signed Into Law." October 15, Pp. 2142. Washington, D.C.: CQ Press.

*Congressional Quarterly Weekly Report*. 1990. "Rethinking The Pakistan Alliance." October 6, Pp. 3238. Washington, D.C.: CQ Press.

*Congressional Quarterly Weekly Report*. 1990. "Retooling Jackson-Vanik." April 28, Pp. 1249. Washington, D.C.: CQ Press.

*Congressional Quarterly Weekly Report*. 1990. "Trade and Foreign Policy: The Ties That Bind." June 9, Pp. 1773-1778. Washington, D.C.: CQ Press.

*Congressional Quarterly Weekly Report*. 1989. "Veto of Chinese-Students Bill Touches Off Furor On Hill." December 2, Pp. 3316. Washington, D.C.: CQ Press.

Cooper, Joseph. 1985. "The Legislative Veto in the 1980s," in L. Dodd and B. Oppenheimer, eds., *Congress Reconsidered*. Third Edition. Pp. 364-389. Washington, D.C.: CQ Press, Inc.

Cooper, Joseph and Patricia Hurley. 1983. "The Legislative Veto: A Policy Analysis." *Congress & the Presidency* 10: 1-24.

Corwin, Edward S. 1957. *The President: Office and Powers 1787-1957*. New York: New York University Press.

Corwin, Edward and Louis Koenig. 1956. *The Presidency Today*. New York: New York University Press.

Crabb, Cecil V. 1976. *Policy-Makers and Critics: Conflicting Theories of American Foreign Policy*. New York: Praeger.

_____ and Pat Holt. 1989. *Invitation To Struggle: Congress, the President, and Foreign Policy*. Third Edition. Washington, D.C.: CQ Press Inc.

Craig, Barbara H. 1983. *The Legislative Veto: Congressional Control of Regulation*. Boulder: Westview Press.

_____. 1988. *Chadha: The Story of An Epic Constitutional Struggle*. New York: Oxford University Press.

Dahl, Robert. 1950. *Congress and Foreign Policy*. New York: Harcourt, Brace and Company.

Deering, Christopher. 1983. "Congress and Foreign Policy: Toward a More Functional Analysis." *Congress & The Presidency* 10: 241-249.

_____. 1989. "Congress, the President and War Powers: Perspectives on a Third Century." CCPS Working Paper presented at the conference on Presidential and Congressional Governance: Cooperation, Conflict and Change. The American University, Washington, D.C. November 8.

Destler, I.M. 1985. "Executive-Congressional Conflict In Foreign Policy: Explaining It, Coping With It," in L. Dodd and B. Oppenheimer, eds. *Congress Reconsidered*. Third Edition. Washington, D.C.: CQ Press Inc.

Destler, I.M., Leslie Gelb and Anthony Lake. 1984. *Our Own Worst Enemy: The Unmaking of American Foreign Policy*. New York: Simon and Schuster.

Dodd, Lawrence C. 1977. "Congress and the Quest For Power," in L. Dodd and B. Oppenheimer,eds., *Congress Reconsidered*. First Edition. New York: Praeger.

Dodd, Lawrence C. and Richard L. Schott. 1979. *Congress and the Administrative State*. New York: John Wiley and Sons.

Donnelly, Warren. 1981. "Weapons: U.S. Nonproliferation Policy in the 97th Congress, First Session." *CRS Issue Brief*. Washington, D.C.: Congressional Research Service.

_____. 1983a. "U.S. Nonproliferation Policy In The Reagan Administration: A Story of Congressional Struggle For Influence." Unpublished Paper.

_____. 1983b. "Congressional Attempts to Influence U.S. Nonproliferation Policy." *CRS Review*. October.

_____. 1983c. "A Preliminary Analysis of the Implications of the Supreme Court Decision in the *Chadha* Case for U.S. Nonproliferation Policy." Unpublished Paper.

_____. 1990a. "India and Nuclear Weapons." CRS Issue Brief. Washington, D.C.: Congressional Research Service.

_____. 1990b. "Pakistan and Nuclear Weapons." CRS Issue Brief. Washington, D.C.: Congressional Research Service.

_____. 1990c. "South Africa, Nuclear Weapons, and the IAEA." CRS Issue Brief. Washington, D.C.: Congressional Research Service.

Eaton, William. 1991. "Senate Likely To Urge U.S.-Soviet Summit Delay." *Los Angeles Times*, January 16, A4.

Edwards, George C. 1986. "The Two Presidencies: A Reevaluation." *American Politics Quarterly* 14: 247-263.

Elliott, William. 1935. *The Need For Constitutional Reform*. New York: Whittlesey House.

Ely, John Hart. 1988. "Suppose Congress Wanted A War Powers Act That Worked." *Columbia Law Review* 88: 1336-1388.

Ethridge, Marcus. 1984. "A Political-Institutional Interpretation of Legislative Oversight Mechanisms & Behavior." *Polity* 27: 340-359.

Fenno, Richard. 1977. *Congressmen in Committees*. Boston: Little, Brown.

Fisher, Louis. 1987. "Judicial Misjudgements About the Lawmaking Process: The Legislative Veto Case," in D. Kozak and J. Macartney, eds., *Congress and Public Policy*. Chicago: Dorsey Press.

_____. 1989. "Legislative-Executive Relations: Search For Cooperation." *CRS Review*. January: 10-11.

_____. 1989. "War Powers: The Need For Collective Judgement." CCPS Working Paper presented at the conference on Presidential and Congressional Governance: Cooperation, Conflict and Change. The American University, Washington, D.C. November 8.

_____. 1991. "War Powers: The Need For Collective Judgement" in James Thurber, ed., *Divided Democracy: Cooperation and Conflict Between the President and Congress*. Pp. 199-217. Washington, D.C.: CQ Press Inc.

Franck, Thomas and Edward Weisband. 1979. *Foreign Policy by Congress*. New York: Oxford University Press.

Fulbright, J. William. 1961. "American Foreign Policy in the 20th Century Under an 18th Century Constitution." *Cornell Law Review* 47: 1.

Fulbright, Hon. J. William. 1967. Remarks in U.S. Senate Committee on Foreign Relations Hearings *U.S. Committments to Foreign Powers* 90th Congress, 1st Session.

Gerstenzang, James. 1991. "Crisis Said Likely To Delay Bush Gorbachev Summit." *Los Angeles Times*, January 15, A 21.

Gilmour, R. and B. Craig. 1984. "After the Congressional Veto: Assessing the Alternatives." *Journal of Policy Analysis and Management* 3: 373-392.

Glennon, Michael. 1984. "The War Powers Resolution: Sad Record, Dismal Promise." *Loyola of Los Angeles Law Review* 17: 657-670.

_____. 1990. *Constitutional Diplomacy*. Princeton: Princeton University Press.

Hamilton, Alexander, James Madison and John Jay. 1961. Clinton Rossiter, ed., *The Federalist Papers*. New York: New American Library.

Hamilton, Lee and Michael Van Dusen. 1978. "Making The Separation of Power Work." *Foreign Affairs* 57: 28.

Hammond, Susan Webb. 1986. "Congress in Foreign Policy," in Muskie, Rush and Thompson, eds., *The President, The Congress and Foreign Policy*. New York: The University Press of America.

Harrison, Glennon J., et al. 1990. "China Sanctions: Some Possible Effects." CRS Report for Congress. March 26. Washington, D.C.: Congressional Research Service.

Hearings Before the Committee on Governmental Affairs. United States Senate, 100th Congress, 1st Session, February 24, 25, and March 5, 1987. Washington, D.C.: U.S. Government Printing Office.

Henkin, Louis. 1990. *Constitutionalism, Democracy and Foreign Affairs*. New York: Columbia University Press.

Huntington, Samuel. 1973. "Congressional Responses to the Twentieth Century," in David B. Truman, ed., *The Congress and America's Future*. Englewood Cliffs, N.J.: Prentice Hall.

Javits, Jacob K. 1987. "The Debate Over the War Powers Resolution," in Michael Barnhart, ed., *Congress and United States Foreign Policy: Controlling the Use of Force in the Nuclear Age*. Albany: State University of New York Press.

Jentleson, Bruce. 1990. "American Diplomacy: Around the World and Along Pennsylvania Avenue," in Thomas Mann, ed., *A Question of Balance*. Pp. 146-200. Washington, D.C.: The Brookings Institution.

Kaiser, Fred. 1977. "Oversight of Foreign Policy: The U.S. House Committee on International Relations." *Legislative Studies Quarterly* 2: 255-280.

Katzmann, Robert. 1990. "War Powers: Toward A New Accommodation," in Thomas Mann, ed., *A Question of Balance*. Washington, D.C.: Brookings Institution.

Kegley, Charles and Eugene Wittkopf. 1987. *American Foreign Policy: Pattern and Process*. Third Edition. New York: St. Martin's Press.

Kingdon, John. 1973. *Congressmen's Voting Decisions*. New York: Harper & Row Publishers.

Kissinger, Henry. 1979. *White House Years*. Boston: Little Brown and Company.

Koh, Harold H. 1988. "Why the President (Almost) Always Wins in Foreign Affairs: Lessons of the Iran-Contra Affair." *The Yale Law Journal* 97: 1255-1342.

_____. 1990. *The National Security Constitution: Sharing Power After the Iran-Contra Affair*. New Haven: Yale University Press.

Lowi, Theodore. 1979. *The End of Liberalism: The Second Republic of the United States*. New York: W.W. Norton & Company.

_____. 1985. *The Personal President: Power Invested, Promises Unfulfilled*. Ithaca, N.Y.: Cornell University Press.

Madison, James. 1987. *Notes of Debates in the Federal Convention of 1787*. New York: W.W. Norton & Co.

Mann, Thomas. 1990. *A Question of Balance: The President, The Congress and Foreign Policy*. Washington, D.C.: The Brookings Institution.

Mayhew, David. 1974. *Congress: The Electoral Connection*. New Haven: Yale University Press.

McCormick, James and Eugene Wittkopf. 1990. "Bipartisanship, Partisanship and Ideology in Congressional-Executive Foreign Policy Relations, 1947-1988." *Journal of Politics* 52: 1077-1100.

McNaugher, Thomas. 1989. *New Weapons, Old Politics: America's Military Procurement Muddle*. Washington, D.C.: The Brookings Institution.

Muskie, Edmund, Kenneth Rush and Kenneth Thompson. 1986. *The President, The Congress and Foreign Policy*. New York: University Press of America.

Neustadt, Richard E. 1960. *Presidential Power*. New York: John Wiley & Sons, Inc.

Norton, Clark. 1982. *Congressional Veto Legislation in the 96th Congress: Proposals and Enactments*. Washington, D.C.: Congressional Research Service.

Paige, Glenn. 1968. *The Korean Decision*. New York: Free Press.

"Panel Subpoenas Nuclear Arms Data." 1990. *Los Angeles Times*, August 21, A20.

Pastor, Robert. 1980. *Congress and the Politics of U.S. Foreign Economic Policy.* Berkeley: University of California Press.

"Percy Worried About Fate of Nuclear Curbs." 1983. *The New York Times,* October 2, A20.

Pregelj, Vladimir. 1989. "Jackson-Vanik Amendment and Granting Most-Favored-Nation Treatment and Access to U.S. Financial Programs To The Soviet Union." CRS Report For Congress. Washington, D.C.: Congressional Research Service.

Pregelj, Vladimir. 1990a. "Most-Favored-Nation Treatment." *CRS Review.* May/June.

_____. 1990b. "Most-Favored-Nation Status for China and the Soviet Union: Procedure for Extending or Denying the Status." CRS Issue Brief. September 12. Washington, D.C.: Congressional Research Service.

Purvis, Hoyt. 1984. "Tracing the Congressional Role: U.S. Foreign Policy and Turkey," in H. Purvis and S. Baker, eds., *Legislating Foreign Policy.* Boulder: Westview Press.

Purvis, Hoyt and Steven Baker. 1984. *Legislating Foreign Policy.* Boulder: Westview Press.

Reagan, Ronald. 1987. Determination Pursuant to Section 620E(e) of the Foreign Assistance Act of 1961, as Amended. Presidential Determination No. 88-4. December 17. Washington, D.C.: The White House.

Reagan, Ronald. 1988. Determination Pursuant to Section 670(a) and Section 620E(d) of the Foreign Assistance Act, as Amended. Presidential Determination No. 88-5. January 15. Washington, D.C: The White House.

Rieselbach, Leroy. 1977. *Congressional Reform In The Seventies.* Morristown, N.J.: General Learing Press.

Ripley, Randall and Grace Franklin. 1984. *Congress, the Bureaucracy, and Public Policy.* Homewood, Ill.: The Dorsey Press.

Robinson, James. 1967. *Congress and Foreign Policy-Making: A Study In Legislative Influence and Initiative.* New York: Dorsey.

Rourke, John. 1983. *Congress and the Presidency in U.S. Foreign Policymaking: A Study of Interaction and Influence, 1945-1982.* Boulder: Westview Press.

Rydell, Randy. 1990. "Opaque Proliferation and the Public Agenda." *Journal of Strategic Studies* 13: 125-151.

Schattschneider, E.E. 1950. *Toward A More Responsible Two-Party System.* New York: Rinehart.

Scheidt, Ann-Marie. 1987. "Introduction," in Michael Barnhart, ed., *Congress and United States Foreign Policy: Controlling the Use of Force in the Nuclear Age.* Albany: State University of New York Press.

Schick, Allen. 1980. *Congress and Money: Budgeting, Spending and Taxing.* Washington, D.C.: The Urban Institute.

_____. 1983. "Politics Through Law: Congressional Limitations on Executive Discretion," in Anthony King, ed., *Both Ends of the Avenue.* Pp. 154-184. Washington, D.C.: American Enterprise Institute.

Schlesinger, Arthur M., Jr. 1959. *The Coming of the New Deal.* Boston: Houghton Mifflin Company.

_____. 1960. *The Politics of Upheaval.* Boston: Houghton Mifflin Company.

_____. 1973. *The Imperial Presidency.* Boston: Houghton Mifflin Company.

_____. 1988. Testimony before the U.S. Senate Special Subcommittee on War Powers, Hearings "The War Power After 200 Years: Congress and the President at a Constitutional Impasse." 100th Cong, 2nd Session, July-September.

Schwartz, Bernard. 1981. "Congressional Veto in the Conduct of Foreign Policy," in T. Franck, ed., *The Tethered Presidency: Congressional Restraints on Executive Power.* New York: New York University Press.

Sinclair, Barbara. 1989. *The Transformation of the U.S. Senate.* Baltimore: The Johns Hopkins University Press.

Smith, Steven. 1989. *Call to Order: Floor Politics in the House and Senate.* Washington, D.C.: The Brookings Institution.

Spanier, John and Joseph Nogee. 1981. *Congress, the Presidency and American Foreign Policy.* New York: Pergamon Press.

Spector, Leonard. 1988. *The Undeclared Bomb.* Cambridge: Ballinger Publishing Company.

Stennis, John and J. William Fulbright. 1971. *The Role of Congress in Foreign Policy.* Washington, D.C.: American Enterprise Institute.

Stern, Paula. 1979. *Water's Edge: Domestic Politics and the Making of American Foreign Policy.* Westport, Conn.: Greenwood Press.

Sullivan, John H. 1987. "The Impact of the War Powers Resolution," in Michael Barnhart, ed., *Congress and United States Foreign Policy: Controlling the Use of Force in the Nuclear Age.* Albany: State University of New York Press.

Sundquist, James L. 1981. *The Decline and Resurgence of Congress.* Washington, D.C.: The Brookings Institution.

_____. 1976. "Congress and the President: Enemies or Partners?" in H. Owen and C. Schultze, eds., *Setting National Priorities: The Next Ten Years.* Washington, D.C.: The Brookings Institution.

Tananbaum, Duane. 1987. "Not For the First Time: Antecedents and Origins of the War Powers Resolution, 1945-1970." in M. Barnhart,ed., *Congress and United States Foreign Policy: Controlling the Use of Force in the Nuclear Age.* (Albany: State University of New York Press).

Tower, John. 1981. "Congress Versus The President: The Formulation and Implementation of American Foreign Policy." *Foreign Affairs* 60: 229-246.

Warburg, Gerald. 1989. *Conflict and Consensus: The Struggle Between Congress and the President over Foreign Policy Making.* New York: Harper & Row.

Weisband, Edward. 1989. "Congress, Codetermination, and Arms Control," in Harris and Milkis, eds., *Remaking American Politics.* Pp. 112-145. Boulder: Westview Press.

Whalen, Charles. 1982. *The House and Foreign Policy: The Irony of Congressional Reform.* Chapel Hill: University of North Carolina Press.

Zablocki, Hon. Clement J. 1984. "War Powers Resolution: Its Past Record and Future Promise." *Loyola of Los Angeles Law Review* 17: 579-598.

# Index